CW00342286

Spotlight on the English Language

A practical approach

Sandy Brownjohn and Gareth Gwyn-Jones

PROPERTY OF
JAMES ALLEN'S GIRLS' SCHOOL
DULWICH SE22 8TE

Hodder & Stoughton
A MEMBER OF THE HODDER HEADLINE GROUP

Acknowledgements

The publisher would like to thank the following for their permission to reproduce copyright photographs in this book:

J Allan Cash Photolibrary p.7; Bridgeman Art Library/Private Collection p.24; Bridgeman Art Library/Formica Ltd, North Shields p.93; The British Library/Oriental & India Office Collection p.56; Central Office of Information p.37 top; Christies Images p.37 bottom; By kind permission of CPC (UK) Ltd p.82 top; E.T.Archive p.12; Mary Evans Picture Library p.22 both; p.23; p.36; p.52 top; Robert Harding Picture Library/Rainbird Collection p.18; Hulton Deutsch Picture Library p.46; p.52 bottom; p.54; p.64; p.73; p.75; p.83; The Mansell Collection p.65; By permission of Mars Confectionery/A Division of Mars UK Ltd p.81; Topham Picturepoint p.58 bottom; Wales Tourist Board p.13; By kind permission of The Archbishop of York p.15 top; York Archaeological Trust for Excavation & Research p.14 bottom.

Every effort has been made to contact the holders of copyright material but if any have been inadvertently overlooked, the publisher will be pleased to make the necessary alterations at the first opportunity.

A CIP record for this title is available from the British Library.

ISBN 0 340 62732 8

First published 1996

Impression number 10 9 8 7 6 5 4 3 2

Year 2003 2002 2001 2000

Copyright © 1996 Sandy Brownjohn and Gareth Gwyn-Jones

All rights reserved. No part of this publication may be reproduced or transmitted in any form or by any means, electronic or mechanical, including photocopy, recording, or any information storage and retrieval system, without permission in writing from the publisher or under licence from the copyright Licensing Agency Limited. Further details of such licences (for reprographic reproduction) may be obtained from the copyright Licensing Agency Limited, of 90 Tottenham court Road, London W1P 9HE.

Typesetting and page design by Mind's Eye Design.

Printed in Dubai for Hodder & Stoughton Educational, a division of Hodder Headline Plc, 338 Euston Road, London NW1 3BH by Oriental Press.

Contents page

The origins of English

English is a mixture of Anglo-Saxon (Old English) and many other languages. But most of the languages that have had an influence on English came from the same beginning thousands of years ago.

Scholars have decided that around 4000 BC there must have been a tribe living somewhere in eastern Europe which spoke a language we now call Indo-European. It is thought that the people from this tribe spread their language over much of Europe, the Middle East and India.

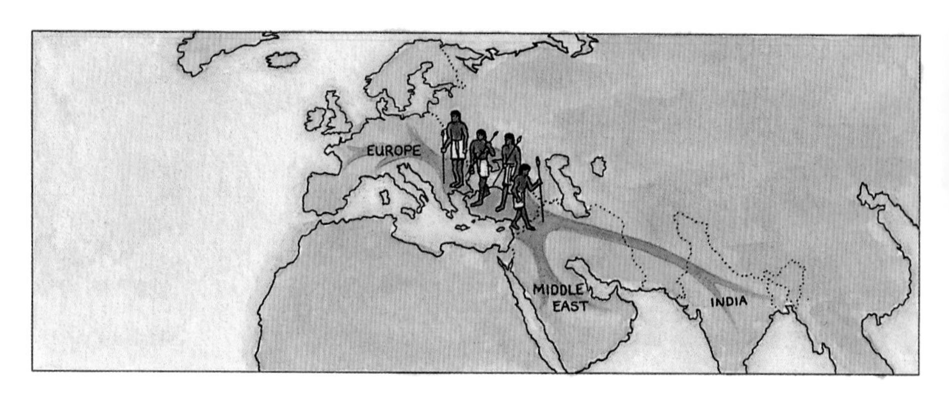

As people moved away and lost touch with the tribe, they developed their own versions of the original language. Words would be invented to describe new objects and situations and, of course, pronunciation would gradually alter in the way it is still changing today. Over the centuries, the language variations became very different.

Around a thousand years ago the Germans spoke a language so similar to that spoken by the English that people were able to understand each other quite easily. Today that is not possible, although there are still many words which are the same or similar:

winter - Winter	summer - Sommer	field - Feld	in - in
to drink - trinken	to sing - singen	long - lang	for - für

How did English develop?

English mainly comes from the Germanic languages brought by the Anglo-Saxons between the fifth and eighth centuries. The Celts and Romans, who came before the Anglo-Saxons, left only a few words - most of them in place names. The Vikings and Normans, who arrived in the eighth and eleventh centuries, brought new words which added to the language rather than changed it.

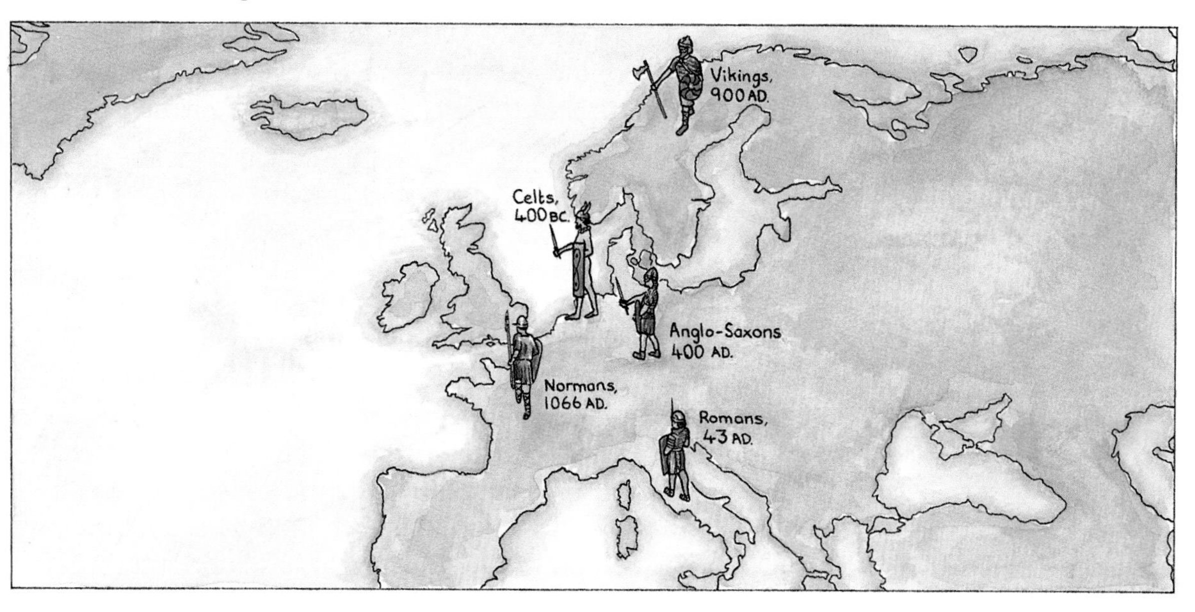

Since then, English has carried on growing. Words have been 'borrowed' from other languages all over the world, and new words have been invented whenever there was a need. Spelling, pronunciation and grammar have gradually altered over the years and continue to do so.

Look at dictionaries in different languages and compare some of the everyday words, like 'father', 'mother', 'land', 'home', 'eat', 'drink' and 'sleep'. Many of the words are almost exactly the same. Where they are different we can often think of other English words which are related, like the French 'dormir' (to sleep) and the English 'dormitory'. Some of your friends may speak different languages and you could make comparisons.

Celts and Romans

The Celts

The Celts arrived in Britain around 400 BC. They were tall and fair-haired, good craftsmen, and fierce warriors. They used iron weapons and easily overcame the farmers who were already there. These shorter, darker people were forced to retreat to the mountains in the north and the west, where some of their descendants still live today.

Brythons and Goidels

There were two main tribes of Celts. The Brythons came from the Netherlands. They settled in the south and west and had kingdoms in Wales and Cornwall. Later, some of them went back to Europe and settled in what is now called Brittany. This is why Brittany's language, Breton, is so similar to Cornish and Welsh. For instance, 'Ty Gwyn' (White House) is a name that can be seen on homes both in Wales and Brittany. The Brythonic word for 'hill' or 'head' is *pen*. This word begins many Welsh and Cornish place names, such as Penmaenmawr and Penzance.

The Goidels were the second main Celtic tribe. They settled in Ireland, Scotland and the Isle of Man. Their language developed into the Gaelic, Erse and Manx languages. The Goidelic word for 'cell' or 'chapel' is *kil*. This word begins many Irish and Scottish place names, such as Kilkenny and Kilmarnock.

The importance of rivers

Water and waterways are very important for life and travel, so river names are amongst the oldest words in English. Many were originally Celtic. For example, the

Cam (at Cambridge) and the Camel (at Camelford) both come from the Celtic word 'cam' which means 'curved and winding'. The following are all thought to be Celtic:

The Avon, Esk, Axe, Exe and Ouse (all mean 'river' or 'water')

The Thames, Tamar, Tame and Teme (all mean 'dark')

The Derwent, Darwin, Darent and Dark (all mean 'oak trees')

THE OLDEST ENGLISH WORDS

The Rivers Severn, Test, Tyne and Humber are just a few of the river names which may come from a time long before the Celts. They are possibly from a language which was spoken by prehistoric man!

The Romans

The Romans occupied Britain for four centuries from 43 AD. The Celtic tribes either retreated to the north or the west where the Romans left them alone, or lived reasonably peacefully alongside their conquerors. Neither mixed much with the other, however, and the Celts mostly carried on speaking their own language.

The Romans, therefore, had little impact on English, apart from several additions to place names and a few specialised words arising from their way of life. For example: *strata* gives the word 'street' and is found in place names such as Streatham, Stratton, Stretton and Stratford; *castra* (Latin for 'a military camp') is found in place names containing *cester*, *caster*, *chester*, such as Gloucester, Lancaster and Colchester. (The first part of these names is usually the original Celtic.)

An excavated Roman road

Look at a modern map of England to find other places which have a form of the Latin word *strata* or *castra* in their names.

Old English

Old English is the name given to the language of the Anglo-Saxons, who first came to Britain in the fifth century. The English we speak today is based on this language. Many modern English words have not changed at all since Anglo-Saxon times. For example:

and we us the to east finger
gold song of from

Others have changed a little but you can see from a few examples how similar they are.

todaeg (today) *hlaf* (loaf) *nama* (name)
faeder (father) *ure* (our) *gelaed* (lead) *forgyf* (forgive)

The shorter the word in modern English, the more likely it is to have come from Old English. All the question words such as 'what?' and 'why?' come from the Anglo-Saxons, although the 'w' and 'h' have changed places in the spelling. Can you work out what the following Old English words mean?

hwaer hwaet hwaenne hwy hwa hwider

COUNT TO TEN IN OLD ENGLISH									
an	twa	thri	feower	fif	syx	seofen	eahta	nigon	ten

Anglo-Saxon literature

English was first written during Anglo-Saxon times. One of their most famous poems tells the story of the hero Beowulf who defeats three monsters - Grendel, Grendel's mother and a dragon.

Beowulf

Try reading the following piece from *Beowulf*. ('sc' is pronounced as 'sh', 'i' as 'ee', and 'ht' as the 'ch' in the Scottish word 'loch').

Com on wanre niht scridan sceadu-genga

It means 'The shadow-walker (Grendel) came shrouded in the dark night'.

Or perhaps you can guess what the verse on the right means - you probably know the modern English version. (þ and ð both stand for 'th')

The Anglo-Saxons used two important writing techniques in their poetry - *Kennings* and *Alliteration.*

Fæder ure, þu þe eart on heofonum, si þin nama gehalgod.
Tobecume þin rice. Gewurþe oinð willa on earðan swa swa on heofonum.
Urne gedæghwamlican hlaf syle us to dæg.
And forgyf us ure gyltas swa swa we forgyfað urum gyltendum.
And ne gelæd þu us on costnunge, ae alys us of yfele.
(about 1000 AD)

Kennings

A Kenning is a descriptive name for something. It is made by saying what the thing is like or what it does. There are usually two words separated by a dash (hyphen). For example:

sceadu-genga means shadow-walker (Grendel);

draca-slaegend means dragon-slayer (Beowulf);

hord-healdend means treasure-guardian (dragon).

You can write whole poems just using Kennings. What do you think the riddle on the right is? Try one of your own and then see if others can guess what you are describing.

Tail-flicker
Fur-licker
Tree-scratcher
Mouse-catcher
Basket-sleeper
Night-creeper
Eye-blinker
Milk-drinker
Lap-sitter
Ball-hitter
Fish-eater
Fire-heater
Wall-prowler
Moon-howler
Cream-lapper
Cat-flapper

Alliteration

This is generally where two or more words, near each other in the poem, begin with the same sound. In this example, Beowulf comes face to face with the dragon.

The **b**reath of the dragon **b**illowed from the rock
In a hissing **g**ust; the **g**round **b**oomed.
It came **f**lowing **f**orward, **f**laming and coiling,
Rushing on its **f**ate.

Try writing your own poem using alliteration. It can be about anything you like.

Days and Months

The days of the week

The English names for the days of the week come from the Anglo-Saxons. They are mostly called after the gods the Anglo-Saxons worshipped before they became Christians.

Monandaeg	the day of the moon.
Tiwesdaeg	the day of Tiw, god of war and the sky.
Wodnesdaeg	the day of Woden, god of war, wisdom and poetry.
Thunresdaeg	the day of Thunor, god of thunder, sky and weather.
Frigesdaeg	the day of Frig, goddess of love and fertility.
Saeternesdaeg	the day of the planet Saturn.
Sunnandaeg	the day of the sun.

Some other nations called their days after Roman gods, but they had almost the same meanings: Mars instead of Tiw; Mercury instead of Woden; Jove for Thunor; and Venus for Frig. They also used Saturn, the moon and the sun.

Look at the days of the week in other languages. Can you tell where they got their names?

The months of the year

The Anglo-Saxon names for the months were mainly based on their farming year and did not survive in English although the words 'month' (monath) and 'Easter' (Eostur) come from them. The English names for the months actually come from the Romans.

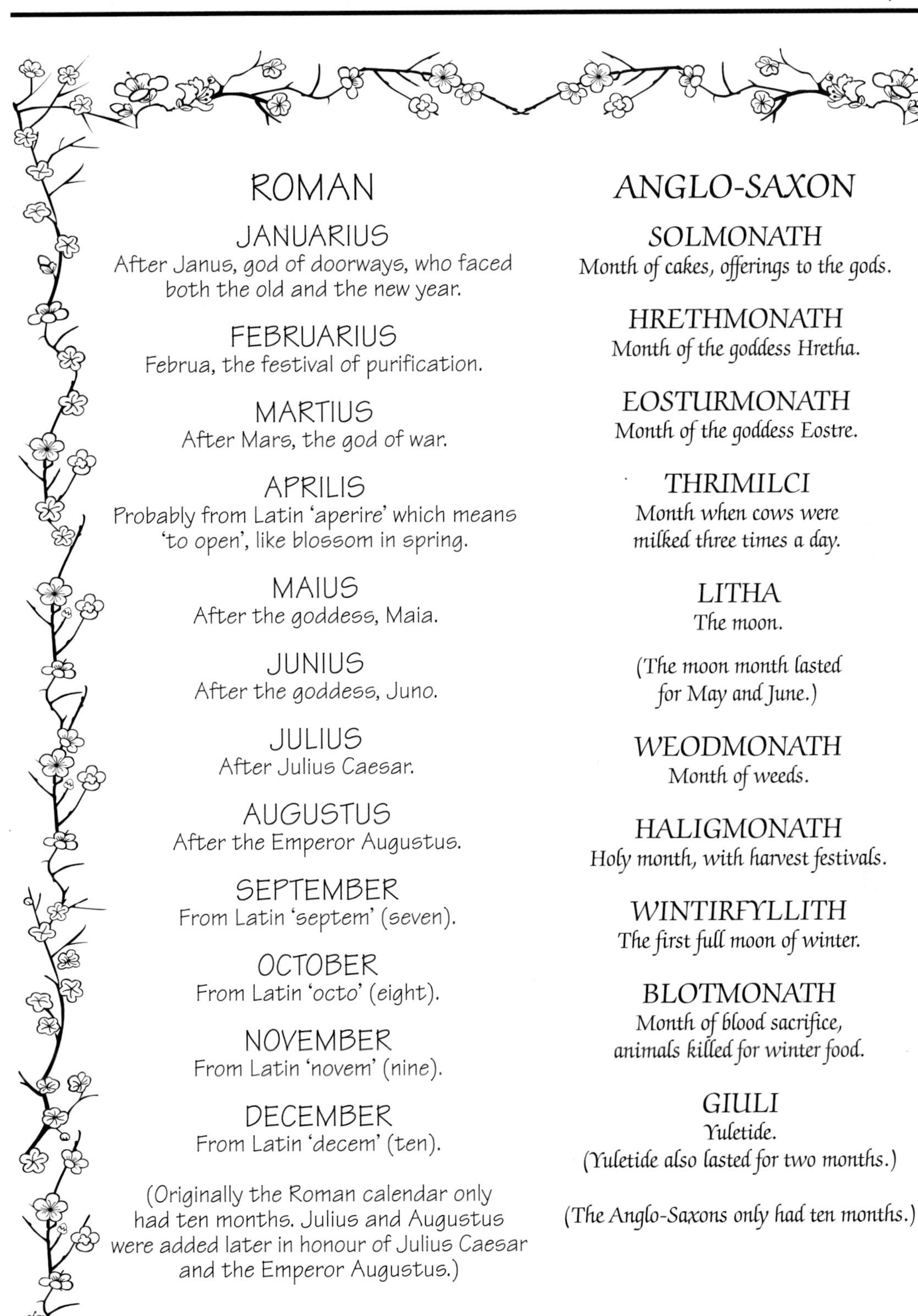

ROMAN

JANUARIUS
After Janus, god of doorways, who faced both the old and the new year.

FEBRUARIUS
Februa, the festival of purification.

MARTIUS
After Mars, the god of war.

APRILIS
Probably from Latin 'aperire' which means 'to open', like blossom in spring.

MAIUS
After the goddess, Maia.

JUNIUS
After the goddess, Juno.

JULIUS
After Julius Caesar.

AUGUSTUS
After the Emperor Augustus.

SEPTEMBER
From Latin 'septem' (seven).

OCTOBER
From Latin 'octo' (eight).

NOVEMBER
From Latin 'novem' (nine).

DECEMBER
From Latin 'decem' (ten).

(Originally the Roman calendar only had ten months. Julius and Augustus were added later in honour of Julius Caesar and the Emperor Augustus.)

ANGLO-SAXON

SOLMONATH
Month of cakes, offerings to the gods.

HRETHMONATH
Month of the goddess Hretha.

EOSTURMONATH
Month of the goddess Eostre.

THRIMILCI
Month when cows were milked three times a day.

LITHA
The moon.

(The moon month lasted for May and June.)

WEODMONATH
Month of weeds.

HALIGMONATH
Holy month, with harvest festivals.

WINTIRFYLLITH
The first full moon of winter.

BLOTMONATH
Month of blood sacrifice, animals killed for winter food.

GIULI
Yuletide.
(Yuletide also lasted for two months.)

(The Anglo-Saxons only had ten months.)

Naming the British Isles

Albion

The Celts gave us the first recorded name for England. 'Albion' probably came from a Celtic word which meant 'the land'. It has often been said that the Romans called the country 'Albus' (a Latin word for 'white') because of the white cliffs they first saw when they came to Britain. But the name had been around long before the Romans arrived. A famous Greek explorer, Pytheas, sailed right round the coast of Britain in the fourth century BC and wrote down many place names of the time. Apart from Albion, there were others such as 'Kantion', which has become Kent. The name Albion, has unfortunately died out and is now only used by poets and football teams.

Britannia

The Romans gave the country the name 'Britannia' after the Celtic tribe of Brythons who lived there. Julius Caesar called these Celts 'Britanni'. (Their cousins, who lived across the Channel in Gaul, gave their name to modern Brittany.)

Nowadays, the word Britain is used for all the countries that make up the British Isles. Britannia is best known as the female warrior who used to be the symbol shown on old pennies. However, it was the Romans who first put Britannia on coins, around the time of the Emperor Hadrian.

England

The name 'England' comes from the Old English (Anglo-Saxon) words *Engla land* which means 'country of the Angles'. The Saxons gave their name to the word 'Sassenach' which is what the Celts called their Saxon enemies. The Scots still call the English 'sassenachs' today.

Wales

'Wales' comes from the Anglo-Saxon word *wealas* which meant 'enemies or strangers'. Wales was one of the areas where the Celts fled to escape the new invaders. However, the Welsh name for Wales is 'Cymru', (pronounced Cum-re) from the Celtic word *cymry* which means 'brotherhood'. This word also gives us the name Cumbria, another area where the Celts gathered.

Scotland

The 'Scotti' tribe were Celts who originally lived in Ireland, which was once called Scotia. They then crossed over to Scotland and gave their name to this land. Before that Scotland had been called Caledonia, and also Pictaria (after another Celtic tribe, the 'Picti').

Ireland

Pytheas recorded the name 'Ierne' or 'Ivernia' after the Celtic tribe of the Eireann who lived there. So, the Romans called it 'Hibernia'. It was the Vikings who gave it the name 'Ireland', which meant 'the land of the Eireann'. The Irish also use their own word, 'Eire'.

Evidence in place names

One of the most fascinating ways to begin a study of the history of English is to look at a map of the British Isles. Place names will show, for example, that the Celts originally entered the country on the eastern side and were gradually pushed north and westwards by later invaders. In the east, East Anglia (the land of the East Angles) has very few completely Celtic names, although some remain, such as the Lynn in King's Lynn, and the rivers Ouse and Cam. Further west and north, particularly in Cornwall, Wales, Ireland, Scotland and the Isle of Man, the majority of place names come from the original Celtic.

Each new wave of invaders from the Continent landed in the east and pushed the local inhabitants west and north. First came the early men of prehistory, followed by the Celts. Then one after the other came the Romans, the Anglo-Saxons, the Vikings, and finally the Normans.

History in place names

The Jorvik museum, York.

Early Celtic names often became so well established that later invaders either left them as they were or changed them slightly to fit into their own language. A good example of how this happened can be seen in the history of the name for the city of York.

The Brythons called it the 'place of the yew tree' – *Evorac*.

The Romans changed 'v' to 'b' and added a Latin ending '-um' – *Eboracum*.

The Angles misunderstood the (still Celtic) name. They thought it sounded like their word for 'village of the wild boar' (eofor) so they called it – *Eoforwic*.

'he Vikings then took that word and spelt it
lifferently – *Iorvik*.

\nd eventually it became – *York*.

Historically, the Church has used Latin and the
\rchbishop of York still signs documents with his
bbreviated Latin name – *Ebor*.)

The Archbishop of York's official signature.

\fter 1066

3y the time the Normans arrived most place names
vere fixed in people's minds. But the Normans, and
ater the Church, often added a second word to the
:xisting name. This might have been the name of a
ocal baron or lord of the manor, or it might show that
he place was part of the nearby monastery or church
ands. For example, the first part of names like Melton
Mowbray, Shepton Mallet and Wootton Bassett is
original English, while the second tells us where the
ord of the manor came from in Normandy. The
Church sometimes added a Latin part which resulted
n such names as Whitchurch Canonicorum
Whitchurch 'belonging to the canons') and Morton
Episcopi (Morton 'belonging to the bishop').

The Normans also added words to avoid confusion
over two places of the same name, such as Stoke Poges
and Stoke Mandeville, and they introduced some of
heir own words, such as 'beau', 'haut', 'bois' and
castle'.

There have been very few new names since the
Norman invasion. Twentieth-century new towns have
usually been given names of existing villages or areas.
One exception is Telford in Shropshire, named after
he famous engineer. Another, much earlier and little
known example, is Baldock in Hertfordshire. This
name was given to his manor by one of the knights
Templar who fought in the First Crusade at the end of
he eleventh century. The name comes from the
Norman word 'Baldac', their version of 'Baghdad'.

Be your own detective

Here are some of the more common words to look for in place names.

Look at the maps of your own area and see if you can work out where the place names come from.

Celtic

Brythonic

avon, afon - river
lan, llan - church
cwm, cum, coombe - a deep valley
lyn, llyn - a lake or pool
pen - hill or head
tre, tref - house or farm
aber - river mouth
dun, din, dinas - fort or town
tor - hill

Goidelic or Gaelic

bal, balla, bally - hamlet or farm
kil - cell or chapel
glen - narrow valley
loch, lough - lake
strath - wide valley
ben, ban - peak
ach, auch - field
bri, brae - hillside
inver - river mouth

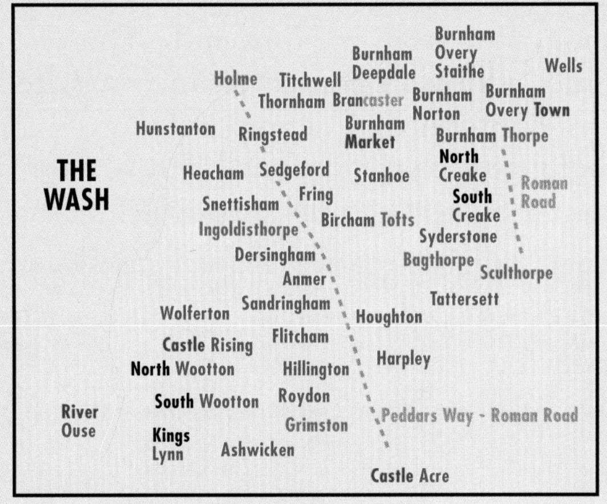

NORTH-WEST NORFOLK - East Anglia
Place names show evidence of each wave of invaders coming from the east.

Roman

cester, caster, chester - from 'castra', a fort or town
coln - from 'colonia', settlement
strat, streat, street - from 'strata', a Roman road
port - from 'porta', a gate
port - from 'portus', a harbour

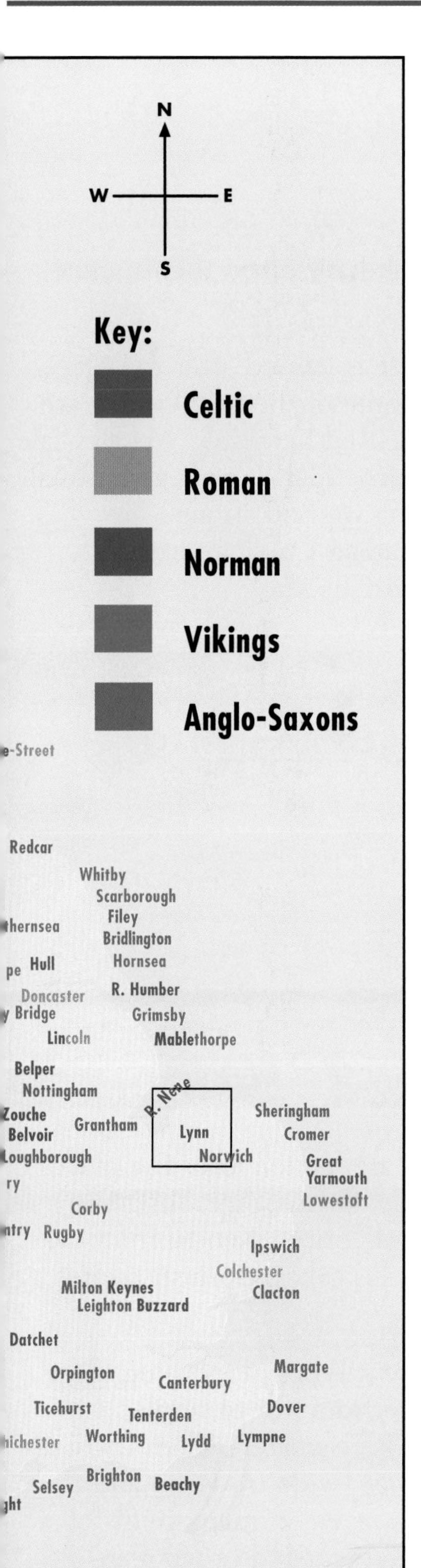

Anglo-Saxon

borough, bury, brough, burgh - from 'burg', a fortified place
hoe, hoo, hough, how - from 'hoh', a rounded hill
ing - from 'ingas', the people or family of...
wick, wich - from 'wic', farm
ham - from 'ham', homestead or village; also from 'hamm', water meadow
ton, tun - an enclosure, farm or village
ey, y - from 'ea', a river; also from 'ieg', an island
leigh, ley - from 'leah', a clearing
stead, sted - from 'stede', a place
stoke, stow, stowe - from 'stow', a meeting place
worth, worthy - from 'worth', an enclosure or farm
field - from 'feld', pasture land; (also battlefield)
den, dene - a valley

Viking

by - a farm or village
thorp, thorpe - a farm or small village
thwaite - from 'thveit', a clearing or meadow
fell - from 'fjall' and 'fell', a steep hill
gill - from 'gil', a deep valley or ravine
kirk - a church
holm, holme - from 'holmr', flat ground by a river, or flat-topped island
garth - from 'garthr', an enclosed space or yard
dale - from 'dalr', a wide valley or dale
ness - a cape, headland

Norman French

Look for words which were added, often unnecessarily, to existing place names by the Normans. For example:

castle abbey tower forest lake river mount market village town

Sherwood Forest - 'wood' and 'forest' mean the same.

Lake Windermere - 'mere' and 'lake' mean the same.

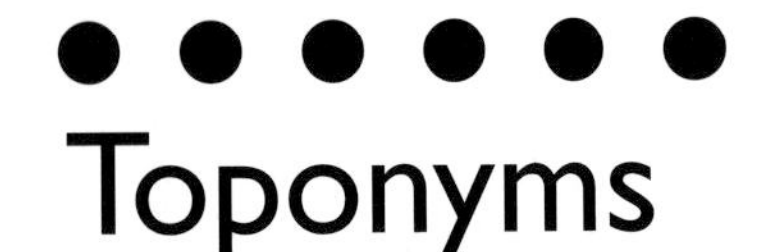

Toponyms

Toponyms are words which have taken their names from places.

Almost every British cheese is named after the place where it was first made. Some of the best known are Cheddar, Cheshire, Stilton, Red Leicester, Wensleydale and Caerphilly. The word 'cheddar' is now given to all cheeses of a certain kind, so we find strange combinations such as Canadian Cheddar, Irish Cheddar and New Zealand Cheddar.

1, 2. Caerphilly and Cheddar
3, 4, 5. Red, White and Blue Cheshire
6, 7. Cream and Curd cheese
8, 9. Derby and Sage Derby
10. Double Gloucester
11. Lancashire
12. Leicester
13, 14. Stilton and White Stilton
15, 16. White and Blue Wensleydale
17. Caboe
18, 19. Orkney and Caithness
20. Cotswold chive
21. Ilchester
22. Red Windsor

Many other famous foods are named after the places where they were first made, for instance, Yorkshire pudding, Pontefract cakes (licorice), Kendal mint cake, Melton Mowbray pies, Eccles cakes, Cornish pasties and Bakewell tarts.

The names of many different types of clothing show where they originally came from: for example, Guernsey, Jersey, and Fair Isle sweaters. Then there are Norfolk jackets, Oxford bags (wide trousers) and the famous Paisley pattern now seen on many items of clothing. The material called worsted (a woollen weave) came from Worstead in Norfolk in the Middle

Ages when East Anglia was the centre of the wool trade. Harris tweed is the woven cloth from Harris in the Western Isles, off the west coast of Scotland. Axminster carpets were originally made in Axminster in Devon.

Dogs, cats, cattle, sheep, pigs and other animals often have names which show where they were originally bred. Some of the best known are: Yorkshire terrier; Manx cat; Hereford, Jersey, Guernsey, Alderney, and Aberdeen Angus cattle; Shetland ponies; and Aylesbury ducks.

Rugger, or rugby football, was the game said to have begun at Rugby, the famous public school.

Newmarket is a card game which takes its name from the East Anglian town of Newmarket, which is famous for horseracing. Interestingly, the same game is played in America but there it is called Michigan.

A Guernsey cow

Toponyms from abroad

Many English words have taken their names from places throughout the world. These are just a few of the most common examples.

'Denim' comes from a place in France and really means the cloth 'de (of) Nîmes'.

'Jeans' takes its name from the Italian town of Genoa, and surprisingly the name has been around in English since Elizabethan times.

'Currant' comes from the Greek town of Corinth. In the Middle Ages in England currants were called 'raisins de Corauntz', which became shortened over time.

'Meander' was originally the name of the River Meander which ran near the famous city of Troy. As the river twists and winds, so meander took on that meaning.

Writing systems and codes

All writing systems and codes are ways of communicating with other people. Often they are used for sending messages. On these pages there are several messages for you to work out. You can also make up coded messages for your friends.

Ogham (or Ogam)

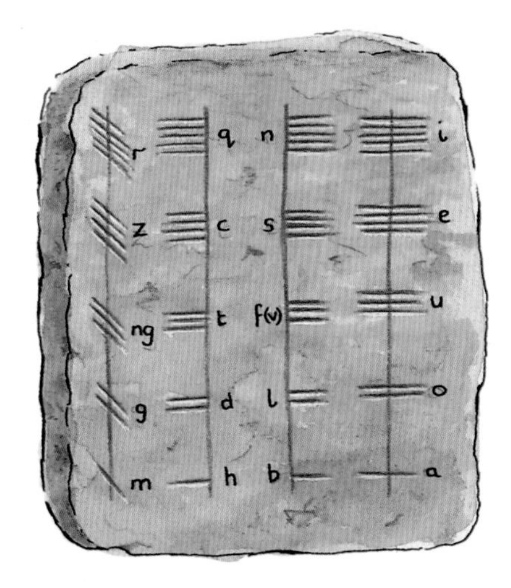

OGHAM

Ogham was used by the Ancient Britons and Irish. It was probably used for sending short messages which were carved on sticks and it has also been found on sacred stones. There were many different versions. Here is one of them. The 20 letters were made by straight lines on a central vertical line.

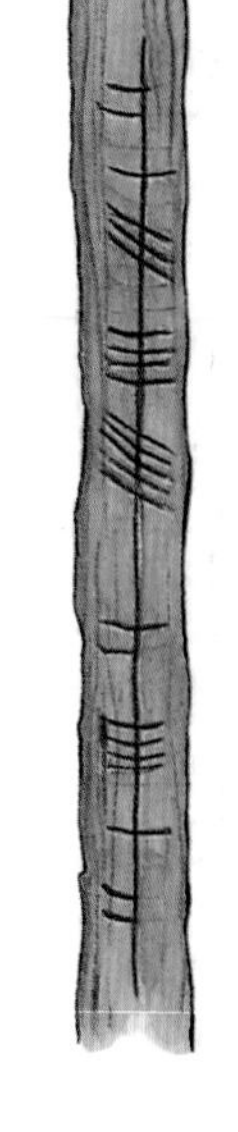

Runes

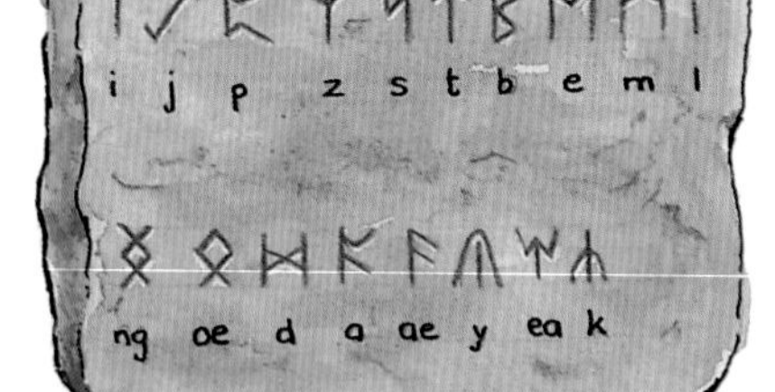

RUNES

The Vikings and Anglo-Saxons brought the runic alphabet, called *futhorc* after its first six letters, to Britain. Some runes were not only letters but were thought to have magic properties.

Morse Code

This was invented in the nineteenth century by an American called Samuel Morse. Groups of dots and dashes stand for each letter of the alphabet. Messages can be sent by radio, *dit* for short sounds (the dots) and *dah* for long ones (the dashes). Morse code can also be signalled by torch using short or long flashes. The morse code call for help is ••• ▬ ▬ ▬ •••(SOS).

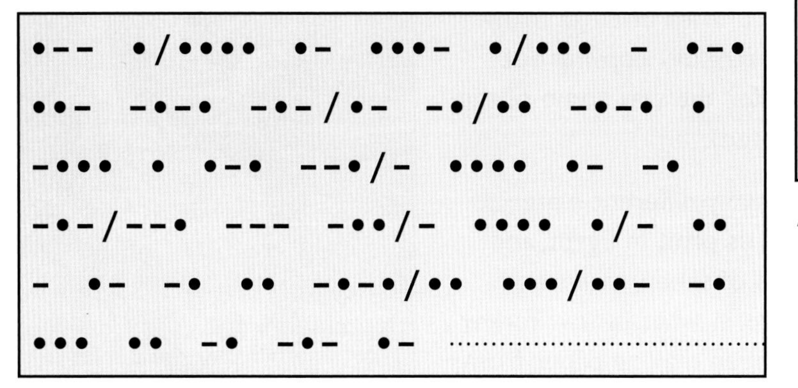

A	•-	N	-•
B	-•••	O	---
C	-•-•	P	•--•
D	-••	Q	--•-
E	•	R	•-•
F	••-•	S	•••
G	--•	T	-
H	••••	U	••-
I	••	V	•••-
J	•---	W	•--
K	-•-	X	-••-
L	•-••	Y	-•--
M	--	Z	--••

MORSE CODE

Semaphore

Semaphore was invented in 1796 by the Reverend Lord George Murray. It was used to send messages over short distances. The signaller held a flag in each hand. The flags were in a different position for each letter. Red and white flags were used on land, red and yellow at sea.

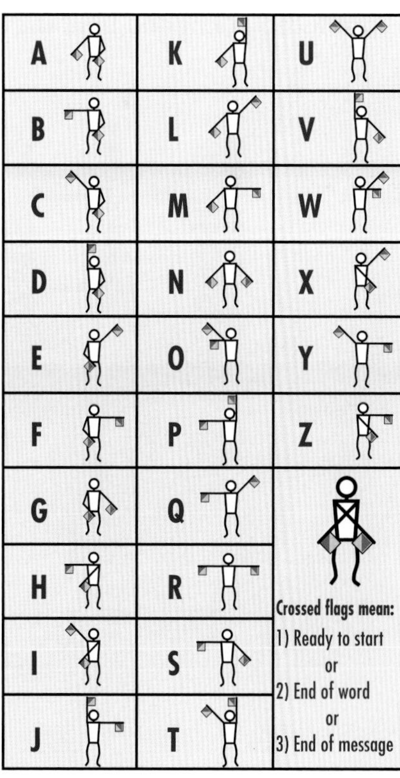

SEMAPHORE

Printing

Before books were printed everything had to be written by hand. Naturally this took a long time and made books very expensive. Not many people could read anyway so it was usually only wealthy people or scholars who owned books. Monasteries had libraries because many monks spent a part of each day carefully copying out books. These books are famous for the way some of the letters were decorated (illuminated).

Before paper, people wrote on many different materials. Silk was used in China, the papyrus plant in Egypt, and parchment (made from the skins of sheep, calves and goats) was invented in Pergamum, in what is now Turkey. Although the Chinese had also been making paper from wood pulp since the second century AD, paper was not produced in England until the fourteenth century.

A mediaeval copyist

A Gutenberg press

The invention of printing

The Chinese invented printing a long time before the Europeans. For centuries they had printed with wooden blocks, but in 1390 they produced the first book printed with moveable metal characters. However, it was 1447 before a German called Johannes Gutenberg built a printing press in Germany along the lines of the local wine presses. This also used moveable metal letters and was quickly copied throughout Europe.

Printing comes to Britain

William Caxton brought printing to England. In 1476 he built the first printing press at Westminster, and in 1477 he produced the first book to be printed in England. He printed a number of books, the most famous of which was *The Canterbury Tales* by Geoffrey Chaucer, in which people on a pilgrimage to Canterbury entertain each other with stories.

William Caxton

Caxton's printing did much to standardise English speech and spelling. He wrote in his own dialect, the dialect of London and the East Midlands, and this was copied by many other printers. However, even Caxton spelt some words in different ways.

The importance of printing

Printed books changed people's lives. More people began to learn to read and school books were printed in English as well as Latin. Within a very short time, just over 100 years, two of the most important and lasting examples of English literature were printed and widely available. The plays of William Shakespeare and the King James Bible both contain some of the best poetry ever written in the English language.

Not everybody welcomed printed books. Up to the early part of the sixteenth century there had been no complete English version of the Bible (see page 73). Now that ordinary people were learning to read, the Bishops were afraid that they would lose control over their congregations and that churchgoers would form their own opinions from reading the Bible instead of from listening to sermons.

Nowadays we take books for granted. Thousands are published every year thoughout the world. But with new technology we can store whole novels on disks or microfiches. Perhaps in time printed books will be considered unnecessary. What do you think?

ABC books

When young children begin the process of learning to read, they are often given ABC books to teach them the letters of the alphabet. 'A was an Archer' is one of the most famous ABC rhymes and was a favourite for illustrated alphabet books for children in the nineteenth century.

A was an Archer, and shot at a frog;
B was a Butcher, and kept a large dog;
C was a Captain, all covered with lace;
D was a Drunkard, and had a red face;
E was an Esquire, with pride on his brow;
F was a Farmer, and followed the plough;
G was a Gamester (gambler), who had but ill-luck;
H was a Hunter, and hunted a buck;
I was an Innkeeper, who loved to carouse;
J was a Joiner, and built up a house;
K was King William, once governed this land;
L was a Lady, who had a white hand;
M was a Miser, and hoarded up gold;
N was a Nobleman, gallant and bold;
O was an Oyster girl, and went about town;
P was a Parson, and wore a black gown;
Q was a Queen, who wore a silk slip;
R was a Robber, and wanted a whip;
S was a Sailor, and spent all he got;
T was a Tinker, and mended a pot;
U was a Usurer (money-lender), a miserable elf;
V was a Vintner (wine-seller), who drank all himself;
W was a Watchman, and guarded the door;
X was expensive, and so became poor;
Y was a Youth, who did not love school;
Z was a Zany, a poor harmless fool.

Anon

The alphabet

The word 'alphabet' comes from the first two letters of the Ancient Greek writing system - *Alpha* and *Beta*.

English uses the Roman or Latin alphabet, so called because it was the Romans who introduced this way of writing to Europe. In Roman times there were only 23 letters (no J, U or W), although the letter 'I' was often written as 'J', and 'V' could also be 'U'. To avoid confusion the J, U and W were added to the alphabet during the Middle Ages. Although there are other alphabets with different numbers of letters, the Roman alphabet is the most widely used in the world today.

English is written using the 26 letters of the Roman alphabet (21 consonants and 5 vowels - a, e, i, o, u), and several different letter combinations to make the other sounds of the language, such as 'th' as in 'there', 'sh' as in 'shut', and 'ou' as in 'out'.

Try writing a modern ABC rhyme. One difference will probably be that more women will feature in your rhyme! Think of the jobs or activities that people do today and use these for your rhyme.
For example:

A is an artist who paints dogs and cats;

B is a builder of houses and flats;

C is a child minder out in the park;

D is a dancer...

You could make an ABC book and illustrate each line.

Alphabet games

There are many alphabet games which are fun to play. On these pages is a selection for you to try out.

Letter riddles (for 2 or more players)

Players take it in turns to ask each other questions whose answers are letters of the alphabet. For example:

Q. What letter can you swim in? A. C

Q. What letter can you drink? A. T

Q. What letter do you play snooker with? A. Q

Q. In which letter would you wait for a bus? A. Q

Q. What letters are very cold? A. IC

Category	Player 1	(SCORE)
Boy's name	Harry	1
Girl's name	Helen	2
Bird	–	0
Flower	–	0
Fruit	–	0
Vegetable	–	0
Fish	Haddock	1
Tree	Holly	2
Animal	Hedgehog	1
Colour	–	0
Country	Holland	1
Town	Huddersfield	2
Author	–	0
Book character	Henny Penny	2
		12

Category	Player 2	(SCORE)
Boy's name	Harry	1
Girl's name	Harriet	2
Bird	Heron	2
Flower	Hyacinth	2
Fruit	–	0
Vegetable	–	0
Fish	Haddock	1
Tree	Hawthorn	2
Animal	Hedgehog	1
Colour	–	0
Country	Holland	1
Town	Hamburg	2
Author	Ted Hughes	2
Book character	Henry (William books)	2
		18

Categories using the letter H.

Categories (for 2 or more players)

Each player writes a list of categories down the left-hand side of a piece of paper. Then each player takes it in turn to choose a letter of the alphabet.

Players must now try to write down something, beginning with the chosen letter, for each category, within an agreed time limit.

When the time is up, each player scores one point for a correct word, even if other people have the same, and two points for a word that no-one else has. (Obviously you score more points if you try to choose more unusual words in each category!)

Letter chains (for 1 or more players)

The idea of the game is to make a chain of words on a theme. Each new word begins with the last letter of the previous word. Try to make the chain as long as possible. The game ends when the chain comes full circle - when the last letter is the same as the very first. If more than one person is playing, the loser is the one who completes the chain.

Noodles - spaghetti - ice cream - mango - onion

Missing vowels (for 2 players)

Each player writes down a well-known saying or proverb, but leaves all the vowels out. (So no 'a', 'e', 'i', 'o', 'u'.) They then swap papers and see who can be the first to put in the correct vowels in order to solve the other's puzzle. For example:

T M N Y C K S S P L T H B R T H

FACT OR FICTION

The wording below is supposed to exist! It is said to have been carved on a church altar many years ago, and gives advice to the Christian congregation.
Can you solve it? You only need to use one vowel (as many times as you like) to make sense of this inscription. It might help you to know that it rhymes. It also contains a couple of words we do not use these days.

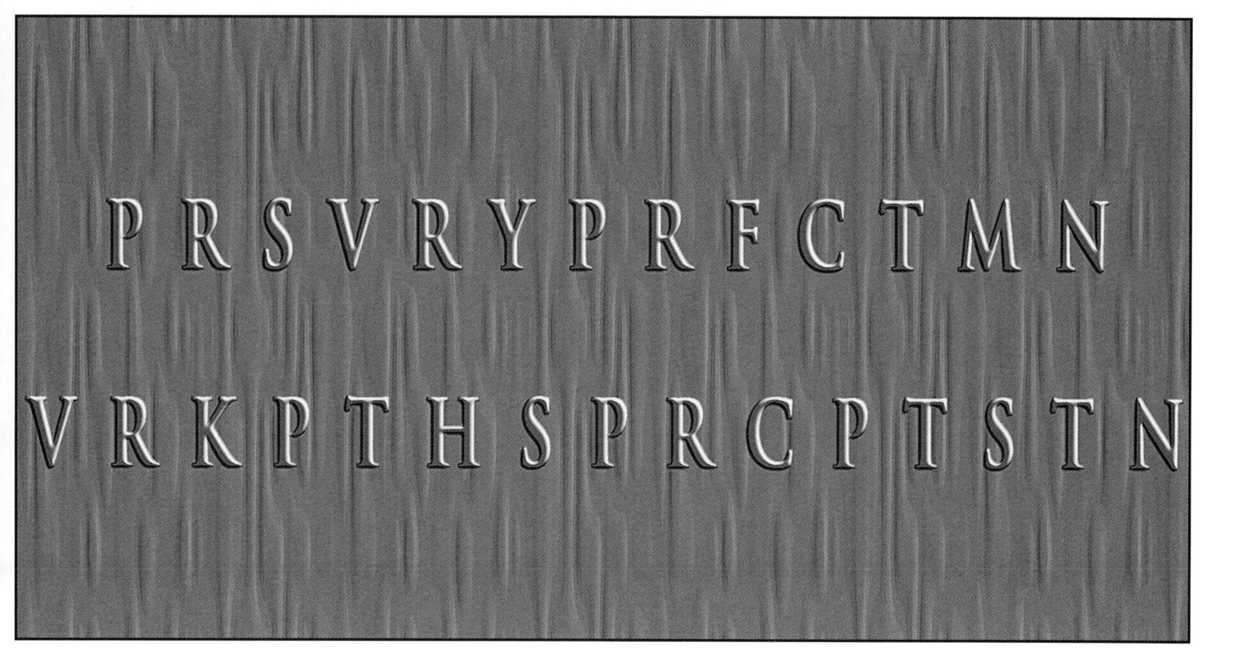

Univocalics

See if you can make up sentences, using words containing only one vowel.

1 Choose which vowel you want to use.
2 Look in the dictionary and make a collection of words with only this vowel.
3 See which ones you can put together to make sense.

For example:

Peg sets her nets wherever she sees eels.

Go to town! - Book now for tomorrow's top pop show.

Fun with parts of speech

All words can be grouped under special names according to the job they do in sentences. There are eight main parts of speech: nouns, pronouns, adjectives, verbs, adverbs, prepositions, conjunctions and interjections. And there are definite ('the') and indefinite ('a' and 'an') articles.

Alphabetical Picnic

This game uses **nouns** (the names of things, people and places). Players take it in turn to say what they might bring to a picnic. Each item begins with the next letter of the alphabet. Every time someone adds something, the whole list must be repeated accurately, otherwise that player is out. When you reach the end of the alphabet, go back to A and carry on until only one person is left. For example:

First player: To the picnic I shall bring some **a**pples.
Second player: To the picnic I shall bring some apples, and **b**iscuits.
Third player: To the picnic I shall bring some apples, biscuits, and my **c**amera.

The Minister's Cat

This alphabet game uses **adjectives** (words that describe something) to describe the Minister's Cat. Each letter of the alphabet is used in turn. (Cheat with 'X'. Use words like **ex**citing, or **ex**cellent.) You will be out if you take too long to think, if you say a word beginning with the wrong letter, or if you repeat an adjective. Go through the alphabet as many times as necessary until there is only one person left in the game, who is then the winner. For example:

First player: The minister's cat is an **a**rtful cat.
Second player: The minister's cat is a **b**lack cat.
Third player: The minister's cat is a **c**lever cat.

Puns with adverbs

Have some fun making up sentences where the **adverb** tells how someone says or does something. The adverbs should suit the sentences in a funny, witty or punning way. For example:

'The garden needs a lot of rain,' she said **dry**ly.
'We're going camping,' they said **intent**ly.
'I want to get to the other side of the road,' said the chicken **cross**ly.

Try these: doggedly, fairly, off-handedly, openly, fruitfully.

Prepositions

Write a description of a place, person or object of your choice using **prepositions** to begin your lines. Use the sort of prepositions which change how you look at something, such as 'over', 'under', 'inside', 'outside', 'around', 'behind' and 'through'. For example:

Under the window is my sturdy bookcase.
Around the window is a white wooden frame.
In the window I can see my reflection.

Interjections

Interjections are exclamations, usually small words like Oh! or Help! and are written with exclamation marks (!). You often find interjections like Kerpow! Yaroo! or Aaaghhh! in cartoons. What do you think might be happening in this story: Pssst! Mmmm! Slurp! Crunch! Ugh! Errghhh! Yuk! Oh No! Help! Mum!

Try writing a story using only interjections! It *is* possible, particularly if you make it into a cartoon strip.

Make your own sentence machine

You will need:

- long cardboard tube (such as the inside of a kitchen roll)
- rectangular piece of card (slightly shorter than the tube)
- sticky tape.

How to make it

1 Cut the card so that it will fit exactly round the tube.

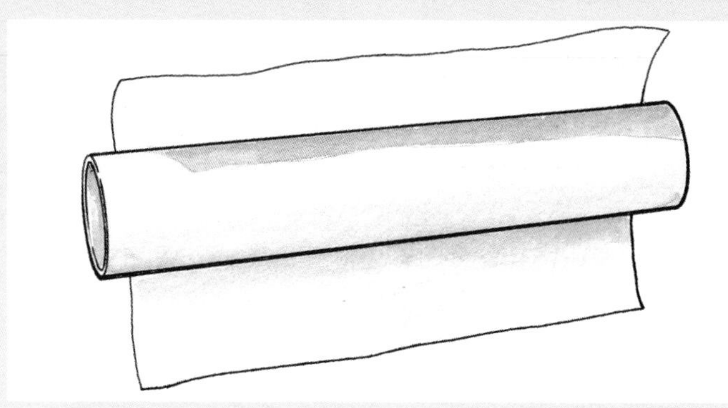

2 Mark out a grid on the card, eight squares across and four squares down.

3 On a separate piece of paper, make lists of the following kinds of words (parts of speech). You can use the ones printed here or choose your own.

Articles	Adjectives	Nouns	Verbs	Prepositions	Articles	Adjectives	Nouns
The	sad	snail	creeps	behind	a(n)	noisy	elephant
A	sexy	sock	flew	over	the	sticky	potato
The	dirty	dog	jumped	into	the	angry	butter
A	yellow	pencil	sings	under	a(n)	naughty	lollipop

4 Write these words into your grid.

The	sad	snail	creeps	behind	a(n)	noisy	elephant
A	sexy	sock	flew	over	the	sticky	potato
The	dirty	dog	jumped	into	the	angry	butter
A	yellow	pencil	sings	under	a(n)	naughty	lollipop

↑ ↑ ↑ ↑ ↑ ↑ ↑ cut up in direction of arrows

5 Cut the grid into strips as shown.

6 Roll each strip, in order, round the tube and join the ends of each one with sticky tape. (Make sure the strips are tight but can still be turned.)

7 Tape rolls of paper or card to each end of the tube to stop the strips falling off.

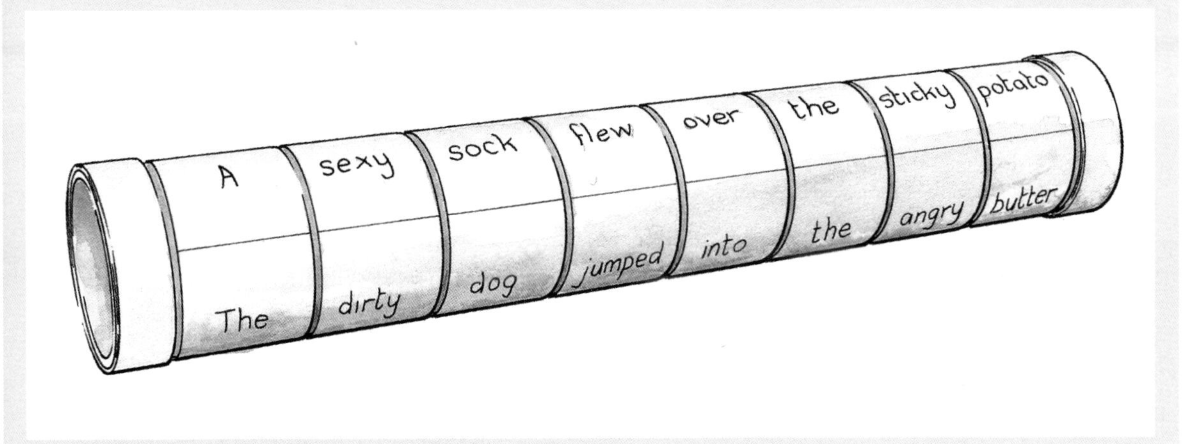

Now turn the strips to see what different sentences you can make. For example:

The sad dog flew into the sticky elephant.

Where do surnames come from?

Richard Smith and Richard Farmer

When did surnames begin?

Surnames, as we know them, did not start until long after the Normans came to Britain. People had names describing what they looked like, where they came from or whose son they were, such as Harold Fairhair, John of Cornwall, or Alfred son of Edmund.

After 1066 many Norman-French names came to Britain. William the Conqueror's four sons were named Robert, Richard, William and Henry. By the fourteenth century seven out of every ten men were called Henry, John, Richard or William. So it became necessary to have a surname to show exactly who someone was, and which family they belonged to.

What do surnames mean?

Our surnames tell us something about our ancestors. Many family names are taken from the countryside or from places such as Wood, Field, Barton, Reading and Cornish.

Jobs make up the largest group of surnames. The most common is Smith. If this is your surname, your ancestors were probably blacksmiths. Every village had its own blacksmith so being a smith was once a very important job. Other job names include:

Miller Butcher Brewer Baker Shepherd Hunter Coward (cow herd) Carpenter Cartwright (cart maker) Tyler Bailey (bailiff) Fletcher (arrow maker)

There are many more. Can you find any from the names of people you know? If they end in 'er', 'smith', or 'wright' they are probably names of jobs.

Hair colour was also popular for names, for example:

Blake (black) Gould (gold) Read (red) Snow

Sometimes people were named after creatures if they seemed to be like them in some way, for example:

Bird Peacock Sparrow Pigge Crabbe Pike

Other names might be a comment on the size or shape of someone, for example:

Long Low Little

Pretty (Old English for 'cunning')

Surnames beginning with Fitz were usually given to someone whose father was from a noble or even a royal family. 'Fitz' meant 'son of' and came from the French word 'fils' (son). However, 'Fitz' also meant that the parents were not married, so the son was illegitimate, as in Fitzjohn or Fitzpatrick. Fitzroy (meaning 'son of the king') was the name given to the illegitimate sons of King Charles II.

Henry Cruickshank and Henry Redhead

Welsh, Scottish and Irish surnames

In Wales, surnames or family names were not widely used until the seventeenth century. However, Welsh families who settled in England took family names just as the English did. Some took the names of ancestors, such as Craddoc, Llewellyn, Morgan or Howell. Others became known by descriptive or nick-names. For example, the Welsh word for grey, *llwyd*, became Lloyd, and *bychan* (little or small) became Vaughan.

Other Welsh surnames were taken from the father's first name, as in Edwardes (son of Edward), Hughes (son of Hugh) and Jones (son of John), or they used the Welsh word *ap* for 'son of' so that ap Owen became Bowen, ap Richard became Pritchard and ap Howell became Powell.

In Scotland and Ireland too, many surnames were taken from the father's name. Mc and Mac at the beginning of a name meant 'son of'.

It is quite possible that you are descended from a famous person in history.

Try drawing your family tree. Start at the bottom of the page with yourself, and any brothers and sisters. Then work upwards as you go back in time.

Collective nouns

A collective noun is a name for a group of things, for example: a herd of cattle; a flock of birds; a school of whales. Most of the collective nouns we use today can be traced back to mediaeval times although many of the most descriptive have unfortunately been forgotten. There are four main types of collective noun.

1 **Ancient phrases** such as a *descent* of woodpeckers, a *watch* of nightingales and an *exultation* of larks.

2 **General terms** such as a *shoal* of fish, a *parade* of soldiers and a *bunch* of bananas.

3 **Single words** made by adding -ery or -age, such as *pottery* (a collection of pots), the *peerage* (Lords and Ladies) and *plumage* (a collection of feathers).

4 **Modern puns** such as a *wince* of dentists, a *rash* of dermatologists (skin doctors), an *odium* of politicians, a *gloat* of examiners and a *dilation* of pupils.

A *shrewdness* of apes

The Church and society in the fifteenth century

In the past the Church affected people's lives far more than it does now. So, it is not surprising that there are a number of collective nouns connected with it. These can tell us a lot about what people thought of those who were in the Church, although you are unlikely to hear them today. For example:

a *scourge* (load or burden) of priests; an *abomination* of monks; a *flap* or a *superfluity* (too many) of nuns; a *decanter* (wine container) of deans.

Other groups of people in mediaeval society also had their descriptive collective nouns, such as a *fawning* (flattering) of courtiers; a *boast* of soldiers; a *faith* of merchants; a *blast* of hunters; a *blush* of boys; a *non-patience* of wives; a *fighting* of beggars.

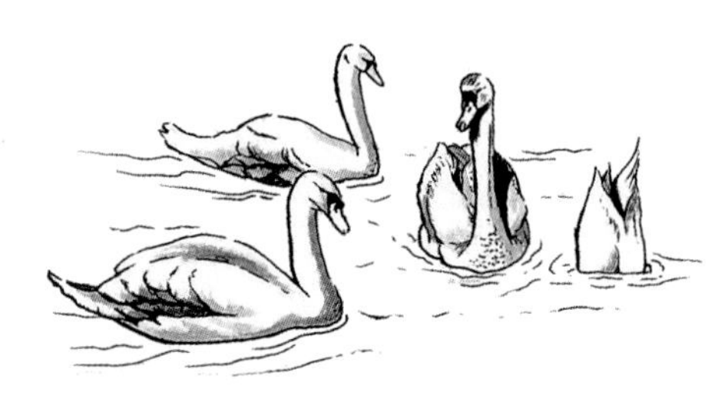

A *wedge* of swans

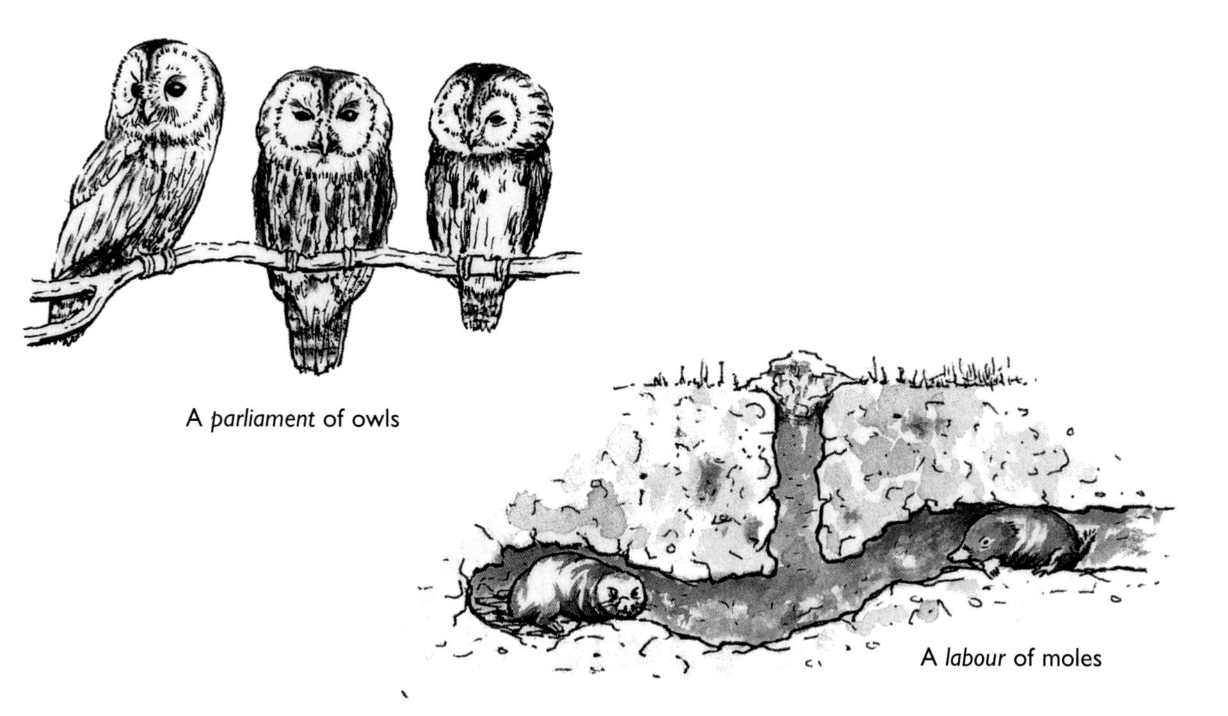

A *parliament* of owls

A *labour* of moles

New collective nouns

When we write stories and poems we should try to invent new phrases and not use ones that everybody knows already. So, practise making up new collective nouns. You may find it easier to do this with a few friends.

1 Decide on the subject for your new collective noun.

2 Then, talk together about your subject. What does it look like? What does it do? Where might you find it? While you are talking, listen for interesting words that could become your new collective noun. The following examples may help you with your ideas:

a *slouch* of snails; a *lag* of tortoises; a *bask* of cats; a *rainbow* of puddles; a *gape* of tunnels.

A *skulk* of foxes

A COLLECTIVE NOUN IN SHAKESPEARE'S *HAMLET*

'To be or not to be: that is the question:
Whether 'tis nobler in the mind to suffer
The slings and arrows of outrageous fortune,
Or to take arms against *a sea of troubles*,
And by opposing end them?...'

Eponyms

Eponyms are new words that come from people's names. They arise because of the way people behaved or the things they did. Below is a selection of British eponyms; some well-known, some less so.

Wellington boots were named after the Duke of Wellington (1769-1852). He was the English general who defeated Napoleon at the Battle of Waterloo in 1815. He and his officers always wore high leather boots which covered the knee in front and dipped down at the back and became known as 'wellingtons'. Nowadays they are made of waterproof rubber and are often affectionately known as 'wellies'.

Sandwiches took their name from John Montague, the Fourth Earl of Sandwich (1718-1792). Actually people had been eating meat between two slices of bread for a long time but it was his actions that gave his name to the practice. He was a notorious gambler and would often remain at the gambling table all night, sending out for snacks of bread with fillings. Thus his legacy to the world became the sandwich. (A group of islands in the Pacific discovered by Captain Cook was also named after him – the Sandwich Islands.)

Cardigan, the knitted woollen jacket, was named after James Thomas Brudenell, Seventh Earl of Cardigan (1797-1868). He led the famous Charge of the Light Brigade in 1854 during the Crimean War, and although the charge resulted in a terrible defeat, Cardigan was considered a hero back in England. The jacket was first worn by British soldiers to keep them warm in the bitter Crimean winter.

Everest, the world's highest mountain (29,028 feet), was named after Sir George Everest (1790-1866) who was the first to produce detailed maps of India and the Himalayas during his time as Surveyor General of India. The word has also come to mean simply 'the highest point'.

Peeping Tom dates back to the year 1040. Leofric, the Saxon Earl of Mercia and Lord of Coventry, was a nobleman in the time of King Edward the Confessor. In order to stop him taxing the people of Coventry, his wife, Lady Godiva, accepted his challenge to ride naked through the streets of the town. All the people were ordered to stay indoors and not to watch, but a tailor called Tom could not resist looking.

Hooligan entered the English language in 1899 when a book called *Hooligan Nights* was published. The author, Clarence Rook, claimed it was based on a real person called Patrick Hooligan who robbed people in the streets. Patrick Hooligan used to visit a Southwark pub called the Lamb and Flag where he controlled a gang of boys who were petty criminals: a sort of real-life Fagin.

Big Ben – Sir Benjamin Hall (1802-1867) was Chief Commissioner of works in London when the great new hour bell for the clock tower at the Houses of Parliament was made. The old one had cracked and the new St Stephen's bell replaced it in 1858. However, the newspapers decided to christen it Big Ben after Sir Benjamin, and so it has remained. Today most people call the whole clock Big Ben.

Teddy Bears got their name from the American president, Theodore (Teddy) Roosevelt (1858-1919). In 1903 Roosevelt went down to the country in Mississippi to hunt bears. The people he was staying with were very anxious that he should be successful, so they caught a small bear, stunned it, and tied it to a tree! Roosevelt thought that this was very unsporting and refused to shoot it. The story was printed in all the newspapers and there was a famous cartoon in the Washington Post. The makers of stuffed toy bears jumped at the chance of turning the publicity to their advantage. Thus Teddy Bear became a household name and has remained so ever since.

● ● ● ● ● ●

What's in a 'nym'?

'Nym' comes from the Greek word *onyma,* meaning 'name'.

Homonyms

Homonyms ('homo' means 'the same' in Greek) are words that have the same spelling and sound the same but have different meanings. For example:

At the end of the trial, the judge spoke at some length before giving his verdict - it was rather a long ***sentence****.*

Doctor Bell fell down a well
And broke his collar bone.
Doctors should attend the sick
And leave the ***well*** *alone.*

Jokes often use homonyms - can you find this sort of 'pun' in any of your joke books?

Heteronyms

Heteronyms ('hetero' means 'different' in Greek) are words that are spelt the same but pronounced differently and have different meanings, such as 'minute' (pronounced 'my-nute') meaning 'very small', and 'minute' (pronounced 'minnit') meaning '60 seconds'. Dictionaries list such words separately - see how many you can find.

Synonyms

Synonyms ('syn' means 'together with' in Greek) are words that have similar meanings, such as 'happy', 'glad', 'pleased', 'delighted' and 'joyful'. You can find lists of synonyms in a thesaurus.

Did you know that there are well over 100 ways of saying 'to speak'? Here are just a few: 'say', 'shout', 'question', 'ask', 'mumble', 'mutter', 'stutter'. See how many you can find and make a wall chart, or a mobile to hang from the ceiling.

You can also try finding synonyms for 'to move'. There are even more of these - over 300!

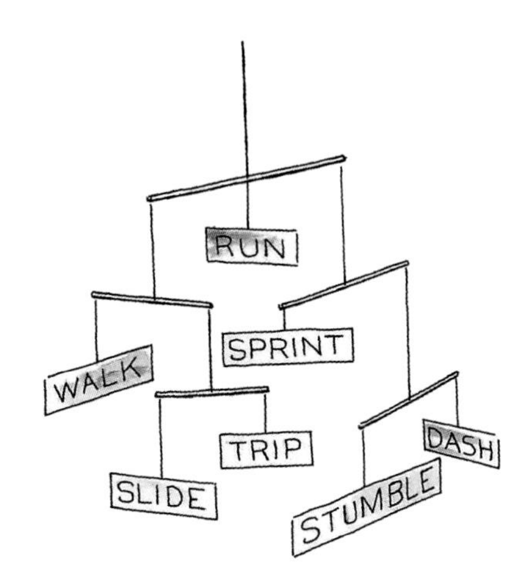

Antonyms

Antonyms ('anti' means 'against' or 'opposite' in Greek) are words that are opposite in meaning, such as 'happy' and 'sad', 'long' and 'short' or 'hot' and 'cold'. You can also find antonyms in a thesaurus.

Make your own antonym card game

This game is played like Pairs, or Concentration. Any number of people can play.

1 Cut up card into 52 equal rectangular shapes. (Alternatively, you can stick your antonyms onto an ordinary pack of playing cards.)

2 You will need 26 pairs of antonyms written, and perhaps illustrated, on your cards. Here are some to start you off.

3 To play the game, shuffle the cards and spread them out face-down on the table. Each player turns over two cards, one at a time, so that everyone can see them. If they are a pair, the player keeps them and has another go. If they are not, they are turned face-down again in their places, and the next player has a turn.

The object of the game is to collect as many pairs as possible.

Breaking down and building up words

Write some haiku poems. Remember that you cannot say very much in only seventeen syllables. You might find it easiest to think of a subject and describe one thing about how it looks or sounds, or what it does.

Syllables

Say your name aloud. How many beats has it? These 'beats' are called syllables and are based on the sounds made by vowels in words. All words can be separated into syllables. How many are in these?

political English rough unsuitability

Some forms of poetry do not use rhyme or rhythm, but have a set number of syllables in each line. One of the best known of these comes from Japan and is called haiku (pronounced 'high-koo'). A haiku has only three short lines. There are five syllables in the first line, seven in the second, and five in the third: a total of seventeen syllables. For example:

Under the front lawn (5)
A mole, with his strong shoulders, (7)
Makes many mountains (5)

Prefix

Dis- in- mis- un- non- (all mean 'not' or 'the opposite of')
as in **dis**agree, **in**direct, **mis**take, **un**able, **non**sense.

ab-	(away, from)	fore-	(ahead, in advance)	pro-	(in favour of)
ad-	(to, into)	in-	(into)	re-	(again, back)
ante-	(before)	inter-	(between)	sub-	(under)
anti-	(against)	mal-	(bad)	super-	(over)
contra-	(against, opposite)	per-	(through)	tele-	(far away)
ex-	(out, away)	peri-	(around)	trans-	(across)
extra-	(more)	post-	(after)		

Prefixes are one or more syllables that go in front of words and change their meaning. Many prefixes come from Latin or Greek words. On the opposite page, are some of the most common prefixes and what they mean. Think of words that begin with some of these prefixes. Can you see how the prefix alters the meaning of each word?

Suffix

Just as prefixes are fixed before a word, so suffixes are put at the end of a word. A suffix changes the way a word is used. For example, one word may take different suffixes, depending on how it is used in a sentence.

Noun	Adjective	Adverb	Verb
ques**tion**	question**able**	questionab**ly**	question**ed**
attrac**tion**	attract**ive**	attractive**ly**	attract**ing**

Here are some of the common suffixes.

Noun endings		Adjective endings		Verb endings	Adverb endings
-er	-ance	-less	-y	-ing	-ly
-or	-ence	-ful	-ary	-ed	
-ure	-ment	-like	-ery	-ise	
-ism	-ice	-ish	-ory	-ize	
-ist	-age	-ent	-ic		
-ship	-ition	-ant	-ous		
-ness	-ation	-able	-ious		
-hood	-ion	-ible	-ive		

A 'root' is the main part of a word. Using both prefixes and suffixes, build on the following roots, which all come from Latin, to see how many words you can make. A dictionary will be very helpful for this.

port (carry) **tract** (draw) **jec** or **ject** (throw) **cred** or **credit** (believe) **pos**, **pon** or **pose** (place or put)

Under the spell

Spelling

Many people say that English spelling is difficult. Well, it is, and it isn't! Actually, only about 400 words that we use every day are not spelt as you would expect, but this is where the trouble lies. Try saying this one:

Ghoti

Now try saying it using the 'gh' from rough, 'o' from women, 'ti' from station.

There are only around 40 sounds in spoken English, but over 200 ways of spelling them! Take 'sh', as just one example.

schedule **sh**ow **su**gar sta**ti**on se**ssi**on o**ce**an **ch**ampagne vi**ci**ous an**xi**ous expan**si**on pre**ssu**re

Can you find words to show the ten different sounds for 'ough'?

Why is spelling so complicated?

The simple answer is that, over hundreds of years, English has grown out of many different languages. All invaders added some of their own words and changed others. And when Britons went abroad, either to fight wars or to trade, they often borrowed words from other countries and languages. The pronunciation of words also changed over time, so that now they may look nothing like the way they are said. It was only about 200 years ago that spelling became fixed - until then the spelling of words did not matter too much, as long as they could be understood.

The great writer, William Shakespeare, did not even spell his own name the same way every time. And, over the years, people have spelt his name in more than 80 different ways! For example:

Shakspeyr	Shaxpere	Shakesper	Shakspeare
Shagspere	Shaksper	Shaxper	Shakeshaft

Since the eighteenth century, many people have tried to simplify spelling. Some of them have been famous writers such as George Bernard Shaw and Sir Arthur Conan Doyle (creator of Sherlock Holmes). However, none of their suggestions or systems caught on. One of the few real successes was in America. Noah Webster, famous for *Webster's Dictionary*, managed to change a few spellings of words such as *theater* (theatre), *traveler* (traveller), and *color* (colour).

Homophones

Words that sound the same but are spelt differently are called homophones. The name comes from the Ancient Greek words *homos* (same) and *phone* (sound). If the wrong homophone is used a passage might be quite difficult to read. However, if you do manage to read it aloud (allowed!), other people will understand it perfectly. For example:

I maid my weigh down the rode. Suddenly eye sore a wight hoarse.

'Ware are ewe off two?' aye asked.

'Too sea the see and watch the son go down.'

'Isle come with yew,' I said.

Sew, I court him and wee road together, wile the wind blue in hour hare.

There are 25 homophones in that passage. Can you find them, and say how the words should have been spelt?

See how many homophones you can find in the dictionary. Make a collection and then write your own story, like the one above, using as many homophones as you can.

A spell of jokes

Puns are jokes which exploit the difference between the way words sound and their spelling and meaning. William Shakespeare was an expert at punning and his plays are full of them.

Make your own joke book

Make your own collection of jokes which can be grouped under the following headings.

Homonyms

Homonyms are words with the same spelling, but different meanings.

Q. Can you **tap** dance?
A. No, I always fall off into the sink.
Q. Doctor, can you make my spots go away?
A. I'm afraid I can't make any **rash** promises.

Homophones

Homophones are words with the same sound, but different spellings and meanings.

Q. What did the brave rock say to the cowardly rock?
A. You should be a little **boulder/bolder**.
Q. Why is the Queen like a storm cloud?
A. They both **reign/rain** over us.

Sounds like...

These can give us some of the worst jokes.

Q. What wobbles as it flies?
A. A jellycopter.
Q. What's green and sings?
A. Elvis Parsley.

Spoonerisms

Spoonerisms get their name from the Reverend William Archibald Spooner, who was warden of New College, Oxford, at the beginning of the twentieth century. He is famous for the way he used to muddle his sentences when he spoke. The first letters of words would be changed round by accident, and become completely different words.

You have **t**asted a whole **w**orm.

Take my umbrella, it's **r**oaring with **p**ain.

He's a **b**oiled **spr**at.

Look for jokes that do the same thing.

Q. What's the difference between a robber and a church bell?
A. One **st**eals from the **p**eople and the other...

Palindromes

Palindromes are words or phrases which read exactly the same backwards as forwards. One of the longest is 'redivider' but there are many three-letter palindromes like mum, dad, nun or bib. There are also palindromic jokes; for example:

Madam, I'm Adam. (said Adam to Eve)

Too hot to hoot. (said by an exhausted owl)

Puns with names

You can have some fun making up book titles and their author's names. You hear the puns when these are read out. For example:

The Broken Window	by Eva Brick
The Haunted House	by Hugo Furst
The Long Distance Runner	by Ivor Stitch

Dear diary...

A diary is a daily record of the events in someone's life. Most people just use a diary to remind them of things they have to do, or events in the future such as the date of their next dental appointment. Some people, however, keep a diary in order to write down the things that have already happened to them, or in the world around them. These are private books where they record exactly what they think and feel, and are not usually shown to other people. Both types of diary, though, can be extremely useful to historians.

Here are some extracts from four famous diaries, all containing people's private thoughts. Two are inventions by authors who have used the diary form to tell stories. The other two are by real people who lived in very different centuries and circumstances. All four, even the fictional ones, tell us much about what life could be like at different times in history.

The diary of Samuel Pepys

Samuel Pepys was born in 1633 and started writing his diary when he was 27. He kept a detailed record of his life for nine years until 1669 when he finally had to stop writing because of bad eyesight. Intelligent and well-educated, Pepys was an important government official and mixed with the rich and famous. He wrote very frankly about his public and private life, and also about important historical events such as the Great Plague and the Fire of London as they were actually happening. He certainly did not want his diary to be read by his family and friends. In order to keep it secret, he used a form of shorthand which was not actually decoded until 1819.

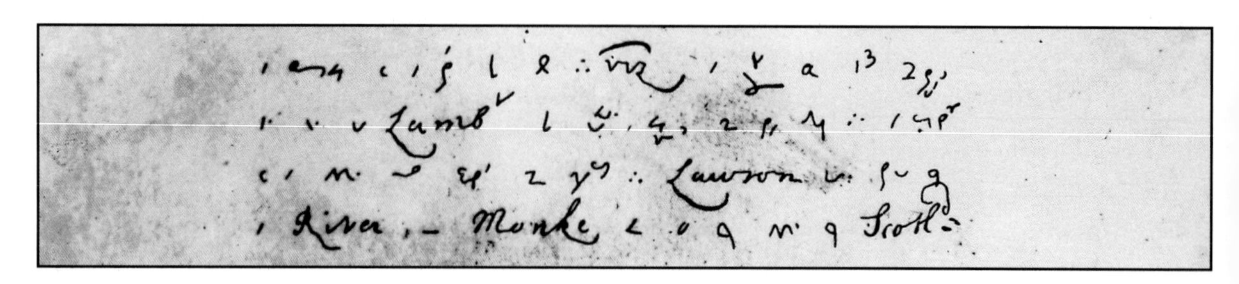

September 1666: The Great Fire. Pepys is watching from the Tower of London.

The houses on this end of the Bridge are all on fire. People are endeavouring to remove their goods and property, throwing them in the river or bringing them off in small boats. Poor people stay in their houses until the fire reaches them. Then they go running and clambering from one pair of stairs by the water side to another. And the poor pigeons are also loath to leave their houses but hover about the windows and balconies until they burn their wings and fall down. As I watch a high and mighty wind drives the fire towards the city and nobody to my sight endeavours to quench it.

The diary of Anne Frank

Anne Frank and her family were Jewish and lived in Amsterdam during the Second World War. When the Germans occupied Holland, Anne's family had to go into hiding because Jews were being rounded up by the Nazis and sent away to concentration camps. She was just 13 years old. For two years, from 1942, her family and four other people lived in sealed off rooms in an office building while friends brought them food. During this time she kept her diary in an exercise book. The final entry was for 1 August 1944. Three days later their hideout was betrayed and they were packed off in cattle trucks to death camps. None of the family survived except her father, Otto. ['Kitty' was the name she gave her diary.]

Wednesday, 13th January, 1943

Dear Kitty,

Everything has upset me again this morning, so I wasn't able to finish a single thing properly.

It is terrible outside. Day and night more of those poor miserable people are being dragged off, with nothing but a rucksack and a little money. On the way they are deprived even of these possessions. Families are torn apart, the men, women and children all being separated. Children coming home from school find that their parents have disappeared. Women return from shopping to find their homes shut up and their families gone.

The Dutch people are anxious too, their sons are being sent to Germany. Everyone is afraid.

The Diary of a Nobody by George and Weedon Grossmith

George and Weedon Grossmith were brothers from a theatrical family who both became famous on the Victorian stage. Their fictional diary of Mr. Pooter was an immediate success and is still thought to be one of the funniest books ever written in English. It was first published in book form in 1892.

Charles Pooter lives a very ordinary life in the suburb of Holloway, London, in late Victorian times. Every day he travels by train to his job in the City. His diary is about the irritations and pleasures, and the family and friends, of a man doing his best to live a dignified and respectable life. We laugh at Mr. Pooter as he faces his everyday problems, but the humour also lies in the fact that we can see ourselves in the same situations.

April 25

In consequence of Brickwell telling me his wife was working wonders with the new Pinkford's enamel paint, I determined to try it. I bought two tins of red on my way home. I hastened through tea, went into the garden and painted some flower-pots. I called out Carrie, who said: "You've always got some new-fangled craze;" but she was obliged to admit that the flower-pots looked remarkably well. Went upstairs into the servant's bedroom and painted her washstand, towel-horse, and chest of drawers.

April 26

Got some more red enamel paint (red, to my mind, being the best colour), and painted the coal scuttle, and the backs of our Shakespeare, the binding of which had almost worn out.

April 27

Painted the bath red, and was delighted with the result. Sorry to say Carrie was not, in fact we had a few words about it.

The Secret Diary of Adrian Mole Aged 13 ¾ by Sue Townsend

Adrian Mole is a teenager who writes a daily account of his fears and feelings. He talks to his diary about his relationships with members of his family, with his friends, with his dog, and with his girlfriend, Pandora.

Adrian thinks of himself as an 'intellectual' and is always writing to the BBC in the hope that his poetic talents will be recognised. He suffers the same worries as every teenager, but, like other teenagers, he feels that he is the first person ever to feel the way he does! He agonises over his parents' embarrassing behaviour, he worries about the shape of his ears or the possibility of his spots getting worse, and he believes that he and Pandora are deeply in love.

Thursday January 1st

BANK HOLIDAY IN ENGLAND, IRELAND, SCOTLAND AND WALES

These are my New Year's resolutions.

1. I will help the blind across the road.
2. I will hang my trousers up.
3. I will put the sleeves back on the records.
4. I will not start smoking.
5. I will stop squeezing my spots.
6. I will be kind to the dog.
7. I will help the poor and ignorant.
8. After hearing the disgusting noises from downstairs last night, I have vowed never to drink alcohol.

My father got the dog drunk on cherry brandy at the party last night. If the RSPCA hear about it he could get done. Eight days have gone by since Christmas Day but my mother still hasn't worn the green lurex apron I bought her for Christmas! She will get bathcubes next year.

Just my luck, I've got a spot on my chin for the first day of the New Year.

Do you keep a diary? It could be very interesting to read later on in life. We forget many things that have happened to us and diaries help us remember.

Interesting facts about English

When William the Conqueror invaded England in 1066 there were only 1.5 million people living there, and they were the only English speakers in the world at that time. Now there are about 300 million speakers of English around the world, and many millions more who use English as a second or third language. In total, English is spoken by around 750 million people - that is almost a quarter of the world's population.

The 20 most frequently *written* words in British English are

the of to in and a for was is that on at he with by be it an as his

All these words are Anglo-Saxon in origin and make up over a quarter of all our reading. Notice that the words 'she' and 'her' do not occur in this list. Can you think why this might be?

The 20 most frequently *spoken* words in British English are

the and I to of a you that in it is yes was this but on well he have for

All these words are also Anglo-Saxon in origin. Notice the differences between the spoken and written English lists.

Can you suggest why these might be? It is interesting to note that the English obviously say 'yes' more than 'no'.

English has the largest and most varied vocabulary of any language in the world. It contains around 500,000 (half a million) words, whereas German has only around 185,000 and French around 100,000. The large number of English words is partly because of the number of different people that have invaded the island. Each invader brought a new language which was added to that already being spoken. For this reason English has a wide variety of synonyms (names for the same thing). For example, there are the general words boat, ship, vessel and craft, not to mention over 200 other names for specific types of boat.

When Sir Christopher Wren finished building St Paul's Cathedral in 1710 Queen Anne came to visit it. She told him that it was 'awful, artificial and amusing'. He was very pleased by this because in those days 'awful' meant 'awe-inspiring', 'artificial' meant 'artistic', and 'amusing' meant 'amazing'.

Every generation has its own particular slang words for things. These are always changing. You can often tell the age of people by the slang they use. Here is a selection of slang words for saying that something is good. Do you, your parents or grandparents use any of them? What's the latest slang word among your friends?

super spiffing excellent wicked awesome brill groovy top-hole fab superb great right-on ripping bitchin' cool well good super-duper fantastic triff marvie rippy first class tip-top topping not bad splendiferous goodgood bad dead good tremendous far-out ace

Words often change their meanings over time. Sometimes their original meanings can be very surprising. For example:

naughty	once meant	'worth nothing or naught'
sly	once meant	'wise'
treacle	once meant	'a wild animal'
pen	once meant	'a feather'
a bonnet	once meant	'a man's hat'

Onomatopoeia is the name given to words that reproduce the sounds of what they are describing, such as 'murmur', 'screech', 'hiss' and 'slurp'.

All the words for the noises that animals make are onomatopoeic as they try to imitate the sounds. For example:

miaow woof quack oink squeak neigh baa moo

These sounds can vary in different languages!

Words borrowed from other languages

Throughout history Britons have travelled to other countries. Sometimes they went to unknown parts of the world as explorers. Sometimes they went to trade. Often they were fighting in wars, ranging from the Crusades in the Middle Ages, through the spread of the British Empire in Victorian times, to the many conflicts of the 20th century. Whenever they came back to England they brought new words which they had 'borrowed' from other languages. Sometimes these new words had passed from one language to another before becoming part of English. And, of course, people coming from other countries to settle in Britain also added some of their own words to the English language.

Missionaries at work in Africa, 1800

During the Blitz (WW2)

The map shows where some of our 'borrowed' words come from. Do you know any more? Some dictionaries tell you a word's etymology (where it comes from).

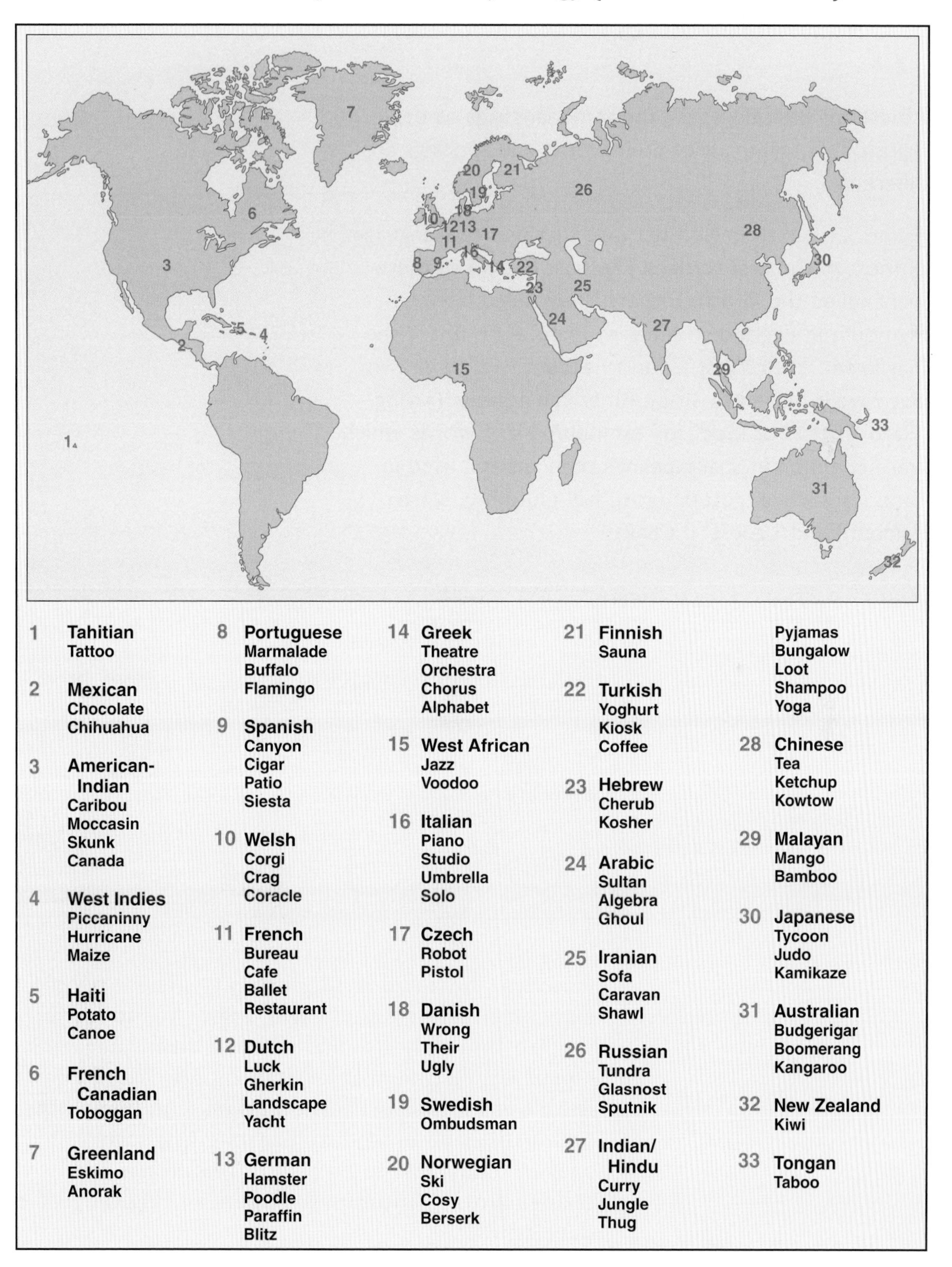

American English

Americans basically speak the same language as the British, although many of their words and spellings are different.

Americans speak English because that was the language of most of the first settlers. The best known of these were called the Pilgrim Fathers. They sailed from Plymouth in England to America in 1620 on board the Mayflower. Their West Country accent with its drawn out vowels helped to shape American accents (saying 'Gard' instead of 'God', for example). Many words which were common in Shakespeare's time are still used in America, such as 'gotten' (got), 'fall' (autumn), 'trash' (rubbish) and 'I guess' (I think).

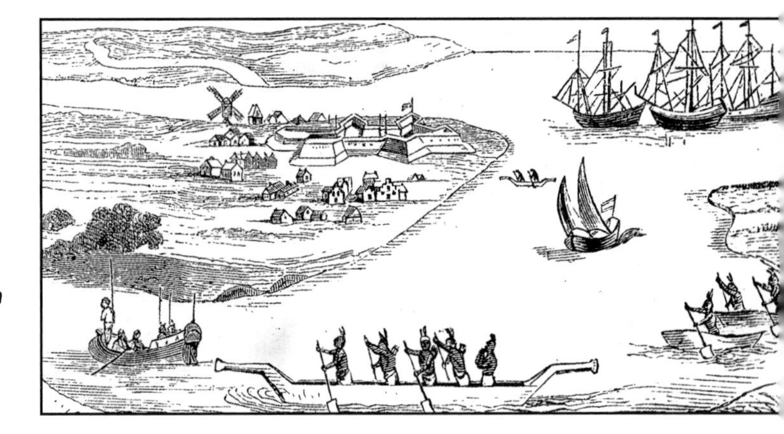

The Dutch colony of New Amsterdam in 1626. The town's name was changed to New York after it was captured by the British in 1664.

Over the following centuries other people settled in America, the 'Land of Opportunity'. These people came from all over the world. Many had to learn English, and they also added words from their own languages. Germans, Poles, Italians, Mexicans, Puerto Ricans, West Indians, Scandinavians, and many other nationalities all helped to form the language that is spoken today. Just as English in Britain has been changing over centuries, so American English goes on developing.

Some differences

Americans use different words from the English for some things. For example, the English say 'tap' while Americans say 'faucet', and the English say 'pants' where the Americans say 'shorts'. But Americans say 'pants' when the English say 'trousers'!

Can you match the following American words with their English equivalents?

The native Americans

Of course, the first people to settle in North America were really the different Indian tribes who arrived thousands of years before the English. They had their own languages but only a few of their words have found their way into English. These were often names of things which were new to the white men and for which they had no words, such as canoe, tobacco, banana, potato and powwow.

The Indians also borrowed some English words into their languages.

What do you think these mean? Say them out loud - it will help you to guess.

Inglisman kabits piks ti timli sanda akson ases azip bastonimoni

Englishman cabbage pigs tea chimney Sunday oxen horses sheep Boston money (American money)

Pidgins and Creoles

Trading ships in the Hooghly, Calcutta, during the 1890s.

Pidgin English

During the seventeenth, eighteenth and nineteenth centuries the British sailed all over the world. They went to trade with other countries and also to conquer them and make them part of the British Empire. Everywhere they went they needed to find ways of talking to the people they met and this was how Pidgin English began.

Pidgin English is not really a language because it does not have rules for grammar or spelling. There are hundreds of different kinds of Pidgin English, as well as various Spanish, French, Portuguese and Dutch Pidgins. Many of them are found in Africa and the Far East. Even today new pidgin languages are born wherever people need to communicate. For example, a Pidgin American English existed for a short while during the Vietnam War in the 1960s.

Nobody seems to know for certain how the word 'pidgin' started. There have been several suggestions. Here are some of them.

- From Chinese mispronouncing the word 'business'.
- From a Hebrew word 'pidjom' meaning 'barter' or 'trade'.
- From a Yao (an oriental language) word 'pidians' meaning 'people'.
- From the English word 'pigeon', something for carrying simple messages.

Each pidgin language is different. Here are a few examples.

From Papua, New Guinea:

gras bilong fes means 'beard' ('grass that belongs to the face');

rop bilong blut means 'vein' ('rope that belongs to the blood').

From the Island of Vanuatu in the Pacific:

Dis smol swain i bin go fo maket;
Dis smol swain i bin stei fo haus;
Dis smol swain i bin chop sup witi fufu;
Dis smol swain i bin chop no noting;
An dis smol swain i bin go wi, wi sotei fo haus.

Can you recognise this well-known nursery rhyme?

Can you match the Melanesian pidgin words on the left to their English equivalents? It will help you to say them aloud. The letters 'ai' are pronounced as 'eye', 'au' as 'ow', and 'ei' as 'eh'.

Creole languages

Creole languages have grown out of some pidgin languages. They developed grammar rules and became languages in their own right. This happened where families began to speak pidgin at home. Creole languages took the place of their own native languages.

ENGLISH ABROAD

Many people abroad actually speak better English than the English do themselves! However, there can be problems. Words in other languages cannot always be translated literally into English. Literal translations do not always say what was really intended.

Japanese road instructions for English-speaking drivers

When a passenger of the foot heave in sight, tootle the horn, trumpet at him melodiously at first,
if he still obstacles your passage, tootle him with vigour, express by mouth the warning Hi! Hi!
Give big space to the festive dog that shall sport in the roadway.
Go soothingly in the greasemud as there lurks the skid-demon.

Notice in a lift in Belgrade

How to operation - Push button of wishing floor. Driving is then going alphabetically by natural order for visiting stations.

Notice in a Belgian luggage department

Hand your baggage to us. We will send it in all directions.

● ● ● ● ● ●

Newspapers

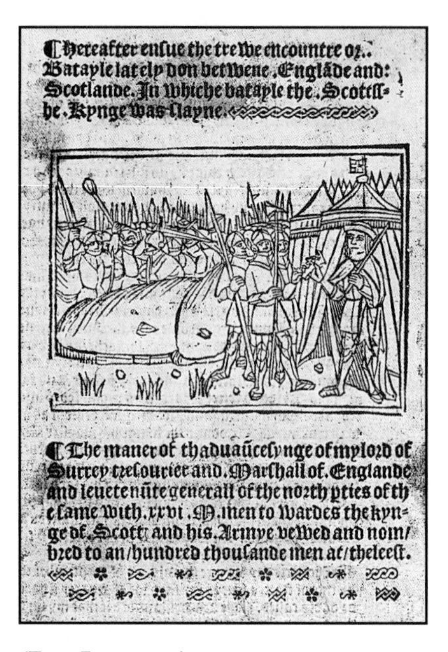

Hereafter ensue the trewe encountre or Batayle lately don betwene Englāde and Scotlande. In whiche batayle the Scottsshe Kynge was slayne.

The maner of thaduauncesynge of my lord of Surrey tresourier and Marshall of Englande and leuetenaunte generall of the north pties of the same with .xxvi. M. men to wardes the kynge of Scottes and his Armye vewed and nombred to an hundred thousande men at the leest.

'True Encounter'

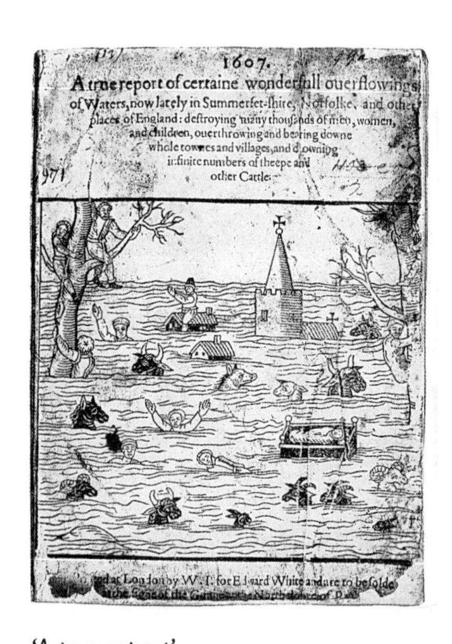

1607.

A true report of certaine wonderfull ouerflowings of Waters, now lately in Summerset-shire, Norfolke, and other places of England: destroying many thousands of men, women, and children, ouerthrowing and bearing downe whole townes and villages, and drowning infinite numbers of sheepe and other Cattle.

'A true report'

The history of newspapers

Possibly the first newspaper ever published was *True Encounter*. This was a pamphlet printed around 1513 giving an eye-witness account of the battle of Flodden. However, for many years most people continued to rely on town criers or travelling ballad singers for their news.

Broadsheets and newsbooks began to be published more regularly in the 1660s. As many ordinary people could not read, the broadsheets usually had woodcut pictures to help to tell the stories.

Many newspapers sprang up during the eighteenth and nineteenth centuries, and almost as many went out of business too. Governments began to raise money by taxing newspapers and advertisements, which put up their cost and made them more expensive to buy. However, some newspapers did manage to survive. On 1 January 1785, *The Daily Universal Register* was published for the first time and went on to become the world's most famous newspaper. We know it today as *The Times*. It was the first paper to have a foreign news service and a reputation for accurate and reliable reporting.

The masthead from an early copy of The Times.

Historical sources

Newspapers are a wonderful resource for anyone studying history. Not only can we read about great events, written at the time they happened, but we can also learn what life was like for the ordinary people. Reports of everyday events, crimes, political changes, sport, entertainment, social events and advertisements - all can help to give us an insight into the lives of people over the last three centuries.

Menagerie.

By the request of several Parties of distinction, the Menagerie, Dale-street, corner of John-street, is reopened, and will continue to exhibit for a short time longer.

By permission of his Worship the Mayor.

NEVER HERE BEFORE.

NOW EXHIBITING, in DALE-STREET, near the Exchange, DRAKE and GILLMAN'S Royal Menagerie and Grand Depot of Animated Nature, never before exhibited in this kingdom, consisting of the most wonderful productions of nature, amongst which are the following:

That stupendous animal the PERFORMING ELEPHANT, from the Theatre-Royal, Covent Garden, London. His astonishing Feats of Performances are as follow:—He opens

The Daily Mirror

THE MORNING JOURNAL WITH THE SECOND LARGEST NET SALE.

No. 2,645. TUESDAY, APRIL 16, 1912 One Halfpenny.

DISASTER TO THE TITANIC: WORLD'S LARGEST LINER SINKS AFTER COLLIDING WITH AN ICEBERG DURING HER MAIDEN VOYAGE.

The beginning of news censorship

When newspapers began, people were able to print whatever they liked. Today, there is an organisation called the Press Complaints Commission which can impose fines on newspapers which print stories that are untrue or unfair to people. In the early days of newspapers there was no such organisation but when Charles I came to the throne, this situation changed.

Charles used a special court called the Star Chamber to stop newspapers printing stories he did not like. If a report offended the king, the Star Chamber took away the newspaper's licence and the printers were often severely punished. They were branded, whipped through the streets, fined heavily or thrown into prison.

WARNING!

Don't believe everything you read in newspapers. Mistakes can be made - both accidentally and on purpose. It is said that if you read a story in a newspaper about something you already know, you will find at least one mistake.

Headlines

Newspapers can be very influential. It is the way stories are written that affects how we see the news. But what makes us read the story is an eye-catching headline. Headlines use different kinds of language to grab our attention. For example:

- Short words P.M. QUITS NO. 10
- Puns GLUE SNIFFERS COME UNSTUCK
- Alliteration FULHAM FANS FORGIVE AND FORGET
- Rhyme VICAR IN KNICKER SCANDAL
- Interjections PHEW! WHAT A SCORCHER!

Journalists write stories in a style that their editors want. They look for particular 'slants' or 'angles' to take as themes for their stories. Different newspapers might report the same story with very different headlines, for example:

BLONDE IN BREAK-IN BACKLASH

SCHOOLGIRL IN PORRIDGE SCANDAL

GIRL CHASED BY WILD BEARS

BEAR NECESSITIES DENIED

CUB LEFT TO STARVE

— BURGLAR — CAUGHT NAPPING

GUZZLING GOLDILOCKS SLEEPS IT OFF

Can you write a report about Goldilocks and the Three Bears, taking your angle from one of these different headlines?

Write amusing headlines for other well-known nursery or fairy tales.

Who does what?

Nowadays, writing for a national newspaper has become quite specialised. All the main newspapers employ the following types of journalists.

Editor-in-chief and Assistant Editor
They are responsible for the overall layout of the paper. They have the final say on what goes in the paper, and where. Other editors report to them.

News Editor and News Reporters
They produce national and local reports for the news section.

Foreign Editor and Foreign Correspondents
They produce reports on news from around the world.

Features Editor and Feature Writers
They produce pieces on anything of interest, including, perhaps, in-depth interviews with people, holidays and travel, the results of surveys, new inventions, health and so on.

Sports Editor and Sports Reporters
They write reports of sporting fixtures, both local and national.

Picture Editor and Assistant Picture Editor
They are responsible for obtaining copies of all the photographs, pictures and cartoons to illustrate the reports and articles. They might also write captions for the pictures.

In addition, people may also be employed to cover the following areas:

- letters page
- births, deaths and marriages
- fashion page
- reviews of TV, radio, films, plays, books, concerts, exhibitions, etc
- advertisements (jobs, items for sale, forthcoming events)
- entertainment listings (TV, radio, cinema, theatre, clubs, etc)
- cartoons
- crosswords and puzzles
- horoscope

A handful of grams

Anagrams

Anagrams are words made from *all* the letters of another word. 'Time', 'emit', 'mite' and 'item' are all anagrams of each other. 'Carthorse' is an anagram of 'orchestra', as are 'her actors', 'other cars', 'chest roar' and 'short care'. How many anagrams can you find for these words:

post star slate miles spear paternal

Pangrams

A pangram is a phrase or sentence which includes every letter of the alphabet. A perfect pangram would therefore have 26 letters, each one used only once. However, this is virtually impossible to do! People learning to type often practise with pangrams, in particular the following one which is the best-known pangram of all:

The quick brown fox jumps over the lazy dog (35 letters).

Try writing your own pangram. It is better to use more letters and make good sense, like these examples.

Pack my box with five dozen liquor jugs (32).

The five boxing wizards jump quickly (31).

Lipograms

A lipogram is a piece of writing which leaves out one letter of the alphabet. Many writers, from the Ancient Greeks onwards, have enjoyed producing lipograms.

You can have fun re-writing well-known rhymes or songs in this way. Only change the words which contain your chosen letter and replace them with a word or phrase which is as near the original meaning as possible. You usually have to lose the rhymes at the ends of lines. Try two or three versions of the same verse, leaving out different letters each time. You will find the thesaurus very useful for this.

This lipogram of a nursery rhyme avoids the letter 'i'.

Three small rodents who could not see,
Three small rodents who could not see,
See how they run, see how they run.
They all ran after Mrs. Farmer,
Who used a sharp steel blade to cut off the long appendages attached to the creatures' bottoms,
Surely, you never saw such an event throughout all your born days
As these three small rodents who could not see.

Telegrams

This is a game in which people make up messages from the letters in a word. There are no real winners, but it is fun to play. Choose the name of a place and write something that could be a telegram message, each word beginning with the next letter of your place name. For example:

HOLLAND	Hope Our Love Lasts And Never Dies.
	Help! Oliver's Lost! Last Appeared Near Dover.
	Had Only Little Luck After Nine Days.

Acronyms

Acronyms is a similar game to Telegrams. (Acronyms are words usually made from the first letters of the title of an organisation or activity, for example: NATO - North Atlantic Treaty Organisation.) For the game of Acronyms, use the letters of a word to write a phrase which tells us something about the word. For example:

mouth	means of uttering to hearers
whales	whopping huge animals living entirely seaborne.

Lewis Carroll (1832-98)

Lewis Carroll is best known for two of his stories - *Alice's Adventures in Wonderland* and *Through the Looking Glass.* The Alice books have become classics and are full of different sorts of wordplay.

Alice with turtle and gryphon

'When we were little we went to school in the sea. The master was an old Turtle - we used to call him Tortoise -'
'Why did you call him Tortoise, if he wasn't one?' Alice asked.
'We called him Tortoise because he taught us,' said the Mock Turtle angrily. 'We had the best of educations. I only took the regular course.'
'What was that?' inquired Alice.
'Reeling and Writhing, of course, to begin with,' the Mock Turtle replied; 'and then the branches of Arithmetic - Ambition, Distraction, Uglification, and Derision.'
'What else had you to learn?'
'Well, there was Mystery, ancient and modern, with Seaography: then Drawling - the Drawling-master was an old conger-eel: he taught us Drawling, Stretching, and Fainting in Coils.'

From the Mock Turtle's Story in *Through the Looking Glass.*

Doublets

Lewis Carroll enjoyed inventing and playing word games like Doublets. To play you need two words which are linked in meaning, such as 'head' and 'tail', or 'top' and 'hat'. You must move from the first word to the second in a series of steps. At each step, one letter only is changed to make a new word. The aim is to reach the second word in as few steps as possible.

TOP to HAT

TOP
HOP
HOT
HAT

(3 or 4 steps:) **cat** to **dog** **head** to **feet** **find** to **lose** **mum** to **dad** **warm** to **cold** **give** to **take** **boy** to **man** **shoe** to **foot**

(5 or 6 steps:) **good** to **best** **wet** to **dry** **hard** to **soft** **easy** to **hard**

New words for old

Carroll's famous poem, 'Jabberwocky' (from *Through the Looking Glass*), is full of invented words.

'Twas brillig, and the slithy toves
Did gyre and gimble in the wabe;
All mimsy were the borogoves,
And the mome raths outgrabe.

'Beware the Jabberwock, my son!
The jaws that bite, the claws that catch!
Beware the Jubjub bird, and shun
The frumious Bandersnatch!'

He took his vorpal sword in hand:
Long time the manxome foe he sought -
So rested he by the Tumtum tree,
And stood awhile in thought.

And as in uffish thought he stood,
The Jabberwock, with eyes aflame,
Came whiffling through the tulgey wood,
And burbled as it came!

One, two! One, two! And through and through
The vorpal blade went snicker-snack!
He left it dead, and with its head
He went galumphing back.

'And hast thou slain the Jabberwock?
Come to my arms, my beamish boy!
O frabjous day! Callooh! Callay!'
He chortled in his joy.

'Twas brillig, and the slithy toves
Did gyre and gimble in the wabe;
All mimsy were the borogoves,
And the mome raths outgrabe.

The Jabberwocky

'Galumph' is what Carroll called a 'portmanteau' word. These are two words pushed together to make one. For example:

'galumph' comes from 'gallop' and 'triumphant'; 'slithy' comes from 'lithe' and 'slimy'. ('Brunch' from 'breakfast' and 'lunch' is a modern example.)

You can make up your own portmanteau words, such as 'dreepy' ('dreamy' and 'sleepy'); 'to grinkle' ('grin' and 'chuckle').

The words 'chortle' and 'galumph', invented by Lewis Carroll, have now entered the English language. You will find them in dictionaries.

History in nursery rhymes

Many of the nursery rhymes we learn when we are very young are based on real people or events in history. Every age produces nursery rhymes though some of them are so old that nobody knows where they come from.

London Bridge is broken down,
Dance over the Lady Lea;
London Bridge is broken down,
With a gay lady.

The first of several London Bridges was built by the Romans and was made of wood. In 1014, at the time of the Saxon King Ethelred the Unready, a Viking raiding party under Olaf the Norseman sailed up the River Thames in longboats. They tied ropes to the timbers of the bridge and then rowed back downstream, tearing the bridge from its foundations. The nursery rhyme is thought to be about this event. (The 'Lady Lea' probably refers to the River Lea which flows into the Thames in London.)

Doctor Foster
Went to Gloucester
In a shower of rain;
He stepped in a puddle
Right up to his middle,
And never went there again.

One possible explanation for the Doctor Foster rhyme comes from the West Country, although why the words 'Doctor Foster' are used, we do not know. It is possible that these were added later just to make a rhyme. Edward I, King of England from 1272-1307, is said to have visited the town of Gloucester when it was so wet and muddy his horse became stuck in the mud. The king looked very undignified, and it took many men, planks of wood and ropes before the horse could be freed. Edward vowed he would never go to Gloucester again.

Ring-a-ring o' roses,
A pocket full of posies.
A-tishoo! A-tishoo!
We all fall down.

Ring-a-ring o' roses refers to the Great Plague in 1664-5. One of the symptoms was a rash of red spots which was the 'ring of roses'. People carried posies and pomanders full of herbs which were supposed to stop them catching the plague. However, if they did become infected they found breathing difficult and they would sneeze. Very soon they would 'all fall down' dead.

'Pop Goes the Weasel' was a very popular song of the 1830s, widely sung in Victorian music halls. To 'pop' was a slang word for taking something to the pawn shop to make some money. A 'weasel' was a tailor's iron which was easily pawned because it was solid metal and therefore of some value.

Half a pound of tuppenny rice,
Half a pound of treacle,
That's the way the money goes,
Pop goes the weasel!

It does not take much detective work to realise that this rhyme could not have existed before the early 1900s. The clue is in the first line! (See page 37.)

Round and round the garden, like a teddy bear;
One step, two steps, tickle you under there!

Nursery and playground rhymes are still invented today. Often, the names of people in the news are included in the verses. This happened particularly during the Second World War when several rhymes made fun of Hitler.

Make up new nursery rhymes of your own about famous people today. Or perhaps you already know some from the playground. You could make a collection and produce a book of twentieth-century nursery rhymes.

Rhyme

When two words sound very similar we say that they rhyme. Our ears pick up the repeated sound. There are several different kinds of rhyme.

Full rhyme is when two or more words have exactly the same sound apart from the first letter(s), as in 'the cat sat on the mat'.

Half rhymes are when words sound almost the same. Sometimes it is the vowels which are repeated, for example: m**u**m and s**u**n. Sometimes it is the consonants, as in pu**ddle** and mi**ddle**.

Rhyme in everyday language

Most people like rhyme because they enjoy the sound. There are many rhyming words which occur in ordinary speech, for example:

helter-skelter   abracadabra   hoity-toity   claptrap

Several of the characters in nursery rhymes, stories and comics have rhyming names, such as Humpty Dumpty, Dennis the Menace and Beryl the Peril. And every year new rhyming words and phrases enter the language.

poop-scoop   wheeler-dealer   fat cat   walkie-talkie

Sometimes the rhyme works by repeating the whole word. These are called **tautonyms**. For example:

goody-goody   yoyo   tomtom   jaw-jaw   gogo

How many rhyming words can you collect?

Rhyming slang

Rhyming slang is really a kind of secret language. It is thought to have been started by Cockneys in London in the nineteenth century. (Traditionally, a Cockney is someone who was born in London within the sound of Bow Bells.) They invented rhyming slang so that they could speak to each other without anyone in authority understanding what they were saying. They replaced the real words with phrases that rhymed. For example:

A *tealeaf* might *half-inch* some *Tom Foolery*.
(A thief might pinch some jewellery.)

Since then, many more phrases have been invented. Often only the first part of the phrase is said, which makes it even more difficult to understand:

He was feeling a bit *Uncle Dick* so he went up the *apples and pears* to rest his *loaf* while his old *Dutch* brought him a cup of *Rosie*.

Can you work out what is being said? What rhymes with the phrases Uncle Dick, apples and pears, loaf of bread, Duchess of Fife and Rosie Lea?

Some expressions we are familiar with today come from shortened rhyming slang, for example:

'take a butcher's' (to look) from 'butcher's hook';
a 'grass' (police informant) from 'grasshopper' (copper).

This is the start of a longer rhyme. What do you think is happening?

I was sitting in front of the **Jeremiah**
A-warming me **plates of meat**,
When there comes a knock at the **Rory O'More**
That made me **raspberry** beat.

I opened the **Rory** and standing there
Was me **one and t'other** - Ted,
Who says, "I'm back from foreign parts."
Says I, "We thought you **brown bread**."

Try writing your own new rhyming slang.

How do you speak?

Accent

An accent is a way of pronouncing words. Everywhere in the world, where English is spoken, there are local accents - as there are, of course, for every language. Most British people can identify the accents of English-speaking Americans, Australians, West Indians, South Africans, Asians or Europeans. It is the music of people's voices that helps us to hear the difference. And all regions of Britain have their own local accents. For example, we can usually tell if someone comes from Yorkshire, Liverpool, Wales, Scotland or Ireland by the sound of the voice.

For example, how do you say the words 'bath' and 'laugh'? In the south of England people say 'barth' and 'larf', but in the north you will hear 'bath' (rhyming with 'math') and 'laff'.

How many different accents are there in your school? Are they all local, or have some people brought accents from other parts of the country or from abroad? Can you imitate certain accents more easily than others?

Tape record people you know who speak in different accents. You could also tape voices from the radio or television to add to your collection. Play these examples to others to see if they can say where the speakers are from. What clues are there to help them guess?

Dialect

A dialect is like a separate branch of a language. It has its own words and grammar, but shares many of the same words with the main language. Every region of the British Isles, and every country in the world where English is spoken, has its own dialect. The picture shows a few dialect words from different areas of England which all mean a 'mid-morning break'.

Standard English

Standard English is the most common English dialect in Britain. It is the dialect we are taught to speak and write in school so that everyone can understand us, regardless of where they are from. Books are also printed in Standard English for the same reason. The spelling and grammar of Standard English is the same throughout the country.

Nowadays, American English, which has some different spellings and grammar, is becoming more widespread internationally and may soon take over as the main English dialect of the world.

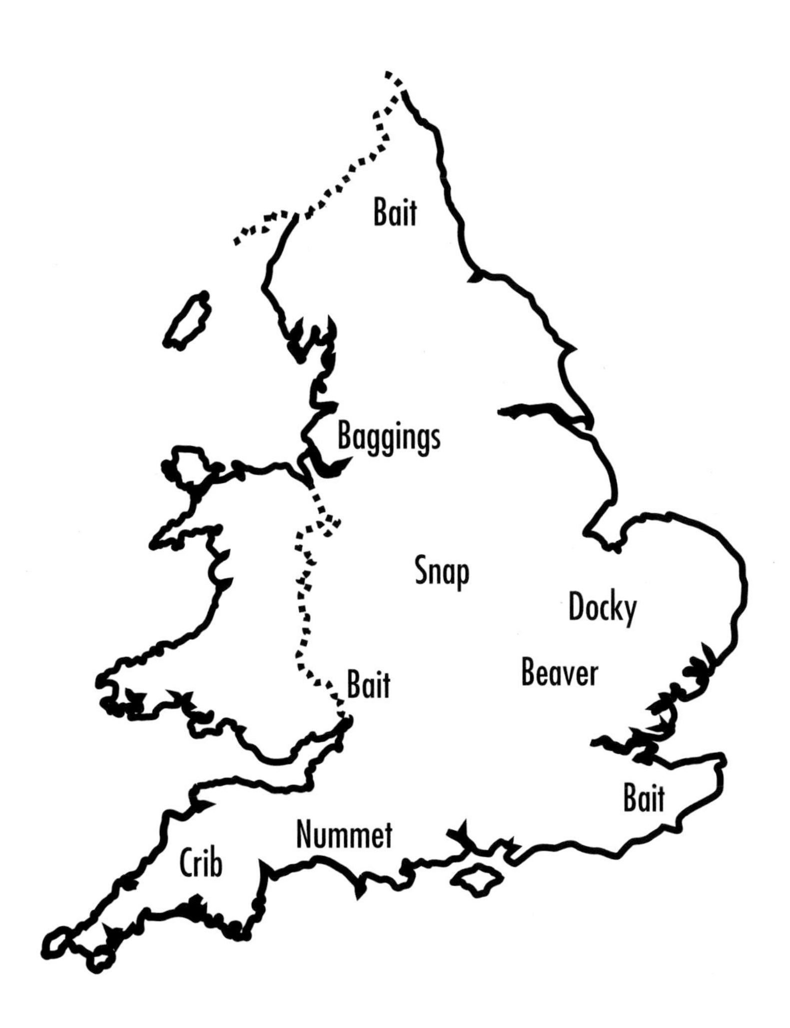

Writing in accents and dialects

When we write stories, poems or plays where people speak in accents or dialects, we have to try to write the words as they sound. Then, we cannot use standard spelling and grammar. Try reading the following extracts aloud.

Write a short scene between two people speaking with an accent or in dialect. It might be the way you, or people in your area, speak. Remember, ordinary spelling and grammar rules do not apply when you are writing in this way.

Man da a England can't even find place fe go.
Most a de time yu hav fe ina house like mouse.
Wen it no too cold it a rain.
Back a yard wen rain start fall
We dis put on som old clothes and gone a mango bush
Or gone ketch janga (river shrimp).
De rain water so warm an nice.
Ova yah man can't mek rain wet dem
Kause five minutes later yu start cough, yu feel chilly;
Baps a cold yu ketch;
If yu no mine sharp it tun ina pneumonia...

From 'When I Walk the Streets' by Fred Williams (born in Jamaica)

'Johnny ont be at school terday cors he hent bin, but iyre give him suffin' ter mearke him go, an' when heer bin, he'll cum.'

A note from a Norfolk mother to her son's teacher

'Shut thi mouth! Shut it can't tha!'
'Come and make me.'
'Tha can only pick on little kids. Tha daren't pick on anybody thi own size!'
'Who daren't?'
'Thee! Tha wouldn't say what tha's just said to our Jud. He'd murder thi'
'I'm not frightened of him.'
'Tha would be if he wa' here.'
'Would I heck, he's nowt, your Jud.'

From A Kestrel for a Knave *by Barry Hines.*
(In Yorkshire, where this extract is set, the letter 'u' is pronounced as it sounds in the word 'put'.)

Wee sleeket, cowrin' tim'rous beastie,
O, what a panic's in thy breastie!
Thou need na start awa sae hasty,
Wi' bickerin brattle!
I wad be laith to rin an' chase thee,
Wi' murderin pattle!

From 'To a mouse' by Robert Burns (Scottish poet 1759-96)

The Bible and Shakespeare

The English language has grown over centuries and has been influenced by many different people. However, there is no doubt that the Authorised Version of the Bible, translated in the time of King James I, and the works of William Shakespeare have played an extremely important part.

Without even realising it, we all know and use words and expressions which appeared for the first time in Shakespeare's plays or in the Bible. When people talk about the 'literary heritage', these are the first two names on the list of great books and authors.

IN* the beginning God created the Heauen, and the Earth.

2 And the earth was without forme, and voyd, and darkenesse was vpon the face of the deepe: and the Spirit of God mooued vpon the face of the waters.

3 And God said,* Let there be light: and there was light.

4 And God saw the light, that it was good: and God diuided† the light from the darkenesse.

5 And God called the light, Day, and the darknesse he called Night: † and the euening and the morning were the first day.

The Authorised Version or 'King James' Bible.

The Bible

The Bible is a book of scriptures (sacred writings). It is in two parts. The Old Testament records the stories, songs and laws of the Hebrews. It is the holy book of the Jewish religion. The New Testament tells of the birth of Jesus Christ, his life and teachings. The Old and New Testament together make the Holy Bible of the Christian religion.

Christianity has been the main religion (whether Catholic or Protestant) in England for hundreds of years, but the first complete English translation of the Bible was not printed until the reign of Henry VIII.

The best known English translation is the Authorised Version, the 'King James' Bible, published in 1611. Although it has a vocabulary of only about 8,000 words, it has given the language many expressions which are still used today. This is partly because until education was freely available to ordinary people, the Bible was the only book they really knew. It is also written in a memorable poetic style.

SOME BIBLICAL EXPRESSIONS	
the skin of my teeth	an eye for an eye
the salt of the earth	a man after his own heart
go from strength to strength	the apple of his eye
in the twinkling of an eye	out of the mouths of babes
the signs of the times	a thorn in the flesh
the land of the living	faith, hope and charity

There have been many more translations of the Bible since 1611 and the most recent are in simple modern language. The aim of these is to make the Bible more easily understood. They certainly make the message clear but lose much of the magic and poetry of the Authorised Version.

You'd better believe it!

Here are the first three commandments translated into the everyday speech of tough New Yorkers by an American prison chaplain.

1. *You shall have no other gods before me...* means God's the leader, nobody, but nobody, man, gets in the way. This is the top. He is Mr. Big, real big.

2. *You shall not make for yourself a graven image...* This means no making things that look like God in the craftshop at the settlement house. No worshipping things like rabbits' foots and lucky dice and, damn it, dolls.

3. *You shall not take the name of the Lord your God in vain...* It means knock off the swearing or you better watch out.

from *God is for real, man* by Carl Burke

William Shakespeare

William Shakespeare was born in Stratford-upon-Avon in 1564, and died there in 1616. For most of his adult life he worked in London where he belonged to a troupe of actors who usually performed at the Globe Theatre in Southwark. He wrote more than 40 plays, of which 38 have survived and are still popular today.

He often acted in his own plays. He also wrote many poems, particularly sonnets.

Shakespeare had a great influence on the English language. He used a vocabulary of over 30,000 words, many of which appeared for the first time in English. He was the first to use in print words such as: accommodation; assassination; countess; laughable; premeditated; dwindle; and fancy-free. He also introduced many expressions which people often use without knowing Shakespeare invented them.

SOME SHAKESPEARIAN EXPRESSIONS

a foregone conclusion
a tower of strength
the darling buds of May
I must be cruel to be kind
at one fell swoop
play fast and loose
the milk of human kindness
in my mind's eye

Saying it by twos and threes

Many of the expressions we use combine words in pairs or threes. Sometimes we want to emphasise what we are saying, and using two or more words in a phrase instead of just one will help to increase the emphasis. For example, the phrase 'hook, line and sinker' means 'completely' but sounds much more impressive. The rhythms of these expressions also make what is being said more interesting to listen to.

Many of these expressions use all sorts of language techniques, as the following examples show.

Alliteration: bits and bobs; signed and sealed; footloose and fancy free.

Full rhymes: thrills and spills; doom and gloom; by hook or by crook.

Half rhymes: time and tide; part and parcel; down and out.

Repetition: by and by; over and over; through and through.

Synonyms: spick and span; leaps and bounds; nook and cranny.

Antonyms: the long and the short (of it)' in black and white; open and shut (case).

Pairs

Match words from the first circle to those in the second to make well-known phrases.

AND

Threes

Three words in a phrase make an even greater impression than two. It is not just the sounds of the words but also the rhythm of the three together. Usually, but not always, the first two words have only one syllable and the last has two. This makes a rhythm that is very satisfying to say. All the language techniques mentioned before can be seen, for example:

stop, look and listen; fair, fat and forty; lock, stock and barrel; healthy, wealthy and wise.

What are the missing last words in these phrases?

Morning, noon and...
Ready, willing and...
Eat, drink and be...
The good, the bad and...
Faith, hope and...
Hop, skip and...
Here, there and...
The truth, the whole truth and...

Here are some famous lines using the pattern of three to make them memorable.

> I'll huff and I'll puff, and I'll blow your house down

the Wolf in *The Three Little Pigs*.

> Friends, Romans, countrymen, lend me your ears

Mark Antony in Shakespeare's *Julius Caesar*.

> In the name of the Father, and of the Son, and of the Holy Ghost

New Testament, Matthew 28, 19.

Oxymorons

Oxymorons are figures of speech which are special pairs of words. They are phrases made of two words whose meanings contradict each other. They are a way of making a description more vivid. One of the most famous examples comes from Shakespeare's play, *Romeo and Juliet*. Romeo and Juliet have just met and fallen in love. Juliet says:

Good-night, good-night! parting is such **sweet sorrow**
That I shall say good-night till it be morrow.

Other examples:

an open secret; a small fortune; bitter sweet; a living death.

● ● ● ● ● ●

Proverbs

A proverb is a saying which tells a truth or gives advice. There are so many of them in English that you can find whole dictionaries of proverbs. There are three main types.

1 Some describe examples from everyday life to suggest what advice is being given. These can be fun to illustrate as they are usually very visual.

Don't put all your eggs in one basket. (Don't risk losing everything at once.)

The gods send nuts to those who have no teeth. (Pleasures and opportunities come too late to be enjoyed.)

2 Some make statements which tell us things which are said to be true all over the world.

Every man has his price. (People will do anything, as long as you pay them enough money.)

Beggars can't be choosers. (You must take what is offered, even if it's not exactly what you wanted.)

3 Others are traditional sayings from folklore, often about health or the weather.

Early to bed and early to rise,
Makes a man healthy, wealthy and wise.

As you probably noticed, proverbs sum up what they want to say in a few words. It often takes many more words to explain exactly what they really mean. Try explaining these:

The early bird catches the worm.

Don't count your chickens before they're hatched.

Sometimes two proverbs cancel each other out with their advice. For example: *too many cooks spoil the broth* and *many hands make light work.*

Playing with proverbs

First, make a collection of proverbs you like. Ask around, and at home. You can also look in a dictionary of proverbs. Then, try making up completely new proverbs on the same sort of patterns as those opposite, for example:

The doorbell always rings for the man in the bath.

Trees offer shade to those who need it least.

When the leaves fall from the trees,
'Tis the time we start to sneeze.

Next, have some fun playing a proverb game. Create new proverbs by mixing together some of those in your collection or slightly changing them. For example:

A rolling stone catches the worm.

He who laughs last goes furthest to the well.

The leopard does not change his socks.

No man is an ice cream.

He who hopes to make hay while the sun shines is only clutching at straws.

These might sound like proverbs but actually mean nothing.

INTERNATIONAL TRUTHS

Different languages often have proverbs which offer the same advice, but through different examples. Ask friends who come from other countries what proverbs they, or their parents, know in their language. Make a collection. Can you explain any of the differences between the following?

English - Every little helps.
French - Little by little the bird makes its nest.
Spanish - Little by little the cup is filled.
Arabic - A hair from here and there makes a beard.
Japanese - Dust may pile to form a hill.
Italian - Feather by feather the goose is plucked.
German - Constant dripping wears away stone.

Advertising

Advertising is a good way of bringing something to our attention. The most common reason for advertising is to persuade us to buy something; either to buy one product rather than another, or to buy something we never knew we needed.

Advertising is all around us. We come across it on television, on radio, in newspapers, on trains, on hoardings, over the telephone, in shop windows, at the cinema, in books and programmes, on clothing and by post (direct mailing). Can you think of any other places where people advertise?

The language of advertising

All sorts of wordplay and language tricks may be used to make us take notice of an advertisement.

- Slogans use repeated phrases that stay in the memory, such as 'The Mint with the Hole' or 'Put a tiger in your tank' (petrol).
- Puns play on the sounds of words and are often found in shop names such as 'Curl Up 'n' Dye' (a hairdresser).
- Misspellings are used to grab our attention, as in 'Kwik Fit' (car repairs), 'Ultrabrite' (toothpaste) and 'Beanz Meanz Heinz'.
- Slang expressions, often using rhyme, are common, such as 'gotta lotta bottle' (milk).
- Visual images are also important and sometimes advertisers can just give us the picture without needing to tell us the name of the product.
- A piece of music often becomes associated with a particular product so that when we hear it we think of that product. Bach's 'Air on a G String', used in adverts for Hamlet cigars, is a good example.

- Adverts based on well-known plays, films, personalities, and even other adverts are also used. These rely on our knowing the original and seeing the funny side of the parody, or 'take off'.

Can you think of other examples for each of these categories?

An advert from the 1950s.

Words to make us buy

Advertisers use some words more than others to persuade us that their product is something we 'must' have. For example:

used by all the top people; hurry while stocks last; new, improved; every home should have one; economy size; the best money can buy; limited edition; special offer; not tested on animals; natural; bio-degradable.

They may try to 'blind us with science', using long technical, scientific and pseudo-scientific language to make us think the product is really up-to-date and special. Examples include: 'dermatologically tested and clinically approved'; 'specially formulated emulsion base'; 'provides deep-down conditioning'; 'hypo-allergenic Anhydrous Lanolin'.

MARMITE is a registered trademark.

Make a collection of adverts from magazines and video some from the television. Look for the different techniques they use to try to sell their product. Are you persuaded by adverts? What makes a successful advert? Are adverts useful and necessary?

Design your own poster or magazine advert. It can be interesting to try to advertise a 'product' which would not normally be sold, for example: 'life', 'worms', 'trees', 'peace' or 'feet'.

The Small Ads

If you look in a local newspaper you will find pages of advertisements for all sorts of things, ranging from cars, houses, plumbing services and pets, to second-hand washing machines and household items. Often, people who advertise in the Small Ads columns use abbreviations to save space (and money). Can you work out what this advert is saying?

FORD ESCORT

1.6i, 16v, 1994 (L), 5dr, 21K, c/l, e/w, fsh, vgc.

£7,100.

Some unusual advertising campaigns

- An optician in Paris once advertised his business by training his cat to sit on his porch wearing spectacles.
- In one American city, where a famous Charlie Chaplin film, *The Gold Rush*, was showing at the cinema, leaflets were handed out promising to pay 1,000 dollars if any one died of laughing while seeing the film.
- A British company recently offered free trips to America to any one who bought one of their vacuum cleaners. So many people took up their offer that it cost the company much more than they made from the sale of the cleaners.

Advertising standards

The Advertising Standards Authority is an organisation set up by the advertising industry itself. It is supposed to make sure that adverts are legal, decent, honest and truthful. Have you come across any adverts that you feel should be banned for any reason?

Dictionaries

A dictionary (or *lexicon*) is a book containing words in alphabetical order. It tells you what the words mean and shows you how to spell them. The more advanced dictionaries will have more information. They tell you which part of speech a word is and how it should be pronounced. They may also tell you where it originally came from - this is called a word's *etymology*.

Samuel Johnson

Famous Lexicographers

(dictionary writers)

The first dictionary was produced by the Chinese in the second century AD. In Britain, people continued to spell words more or less as they wished until a number of English dictionaries were printed in the eighteenth century. The most famous was the *Dictionary of the English Language* produced by Dr Samuel Johnson in 1755. It took him seven years to write. At last people had a book which listed both words and their meanings, and which began to establish standard spellings for all words.

Two other men helped to ensure that English now has the finest dictionaries in the world. Noah Webster, the American lexicographer, published his *American Dictionary of the English Language* in 1828. James Murray, a Scot, became the editor of *The Oxford English Dictionary* in 1879. The first volume was published in 1884 but it took 44 years and many helpers before all twelve were finished. Murray actually died in 1915, long before it was completed. Both the *OED* and Webster's dictionary became the most important reference books for English and American English.

Alphabetical Collection

A B C D E F G H I

J K L M N O P Q R

S T U V W X Y Z

How many words of two or more letters, with all the letters in alphabetical order, can you find?

For example:

with no double letters:

b-e-l-o-w g-l-o-r-y c-h-i-n-t-z

with double letters:

b-e-l-l-o-w l-o-o-p-s k-n-o-t-t-y

What is the longest word you can find?

The dictionary will help you to find these words.

Letters

Most people, at some time in their lives, write letters. We can learn a lot from people's letters about what life was like at different times in history. We can also see how language has changed over the years. Here are a few letters written by very different sorts of people, and for very different reasons.

Sir Philip Sidney was a politician and soldier who served Queen Elizabeth I. This is part of a letter he wrote to her in 1585. In those days it was quite usual for people to spell as they wished.

Most gratious soverein.

This rude peece of paper shall presume becaws of your Majesties commandement, most humbly to present such a cypher as little leysure coold afoord me... I most lowly kiss your handes and prai to God your enemies mai then onely have peece when thei are weery of knowing your force. At Gravesend this 10th November.

Your Majesties most humble servant.

Ph Sidnei

To the Queenes most
Excellent Majesty

When the writer Thomas Chatterton was only 18 years old, a woman called Esther Saunders read some of his poems and fell in love with him. She wrote him the following letter. Her use of language tells us a lot about her.

Sir

to a blage you I wright a few Lines to you But have not the weakness to be Believe all you Say of me for you may Say as much to other young ladys for all I kno But I Cant go out of a Sunday with you for I ham a fraid we Shall be Seen to go Sir if it agreeable to you I had Take a walk with you in the morning for I be Belive we Shant be Seen a bout 6 a clock But we must wait with patient for ther is a Time for all things.

April 3 1770

Esther Saunders

Chatterton replied as follows.

There is a time for all things - Except Marriage my dear.
And so your humble Servant
T. Chatterton
April 9th-

CHOLERA AND WATER.
BOARD OF WORKS
FOR THE LIMEHOUSE DISTRICT
Comprising Limehouse, Ratcliff, Shadwell and Wapping.
The INHABITANTS of the District within which CHOLERA IS PREVAILING, are earnestly advised
NOT TO DRINK ANY WATER
WHICH HAS NOT PREVIOUSLY BEEN BOILED
Fresh Water ought to be Boiled every Morning for the day's use, and what remains of it ought to be thrown away at night. The Water ought not to stand where any kind of dirt can get into it, and great care ought to be given to see that Water Butts and Cisterns are free from dirt.
BY ORDER, THOS. W. RATCLIFF CLERK OF THE BOARD

The Times newspaper is famous for its Letters column. People write about all sorts of topics. The letter below, written in the nineteenth century, is from a group of people who lived in a slum area of London.

Sur, may we beg and beseech your proteckshion and power... we live in muck and filthe. We aint got no privy, no dust bins, no drains, no water supplies... if the Colera comes Lord help us...

This letter, written in 1937, is about a very different matter.

26th April 1937

Sir,

In The Times of 22 April it was stated that a singing mouse had been found in Wales and that it is to broadcast on 8 May.

It may interest your readers to know that, according to Red Indian mythology, 'Mish-a-boh-quas', the singing mouse, always comes to tell of war.

It may sing at other times but not to the same extent.

I read this in Ernest Thompson Seton's wonderful book Rolf in the Woods.

I am your obedient servant,

Alison Holmes

When did you last write a letter?

Write a letter to someone famous. If you and your friends write to different people, it will be interesting to see who replies and to compare what they say. Remember to enclose a stamped envelope addressed to yourself - you are more likely to receive an answer that way.

Parody, pastiche and style

We four lads of Liverpool are,
John in a taxi, Paul in a car,
George on a scooter, beeping his hooter
Following Ringo Starr.

(1960s playground rhyme about the Beatles – a parody of the carol, 'We three kings of Orient are'.)

Parody is an imitation of someone else's work and usually makes fun of the original. Parodies work best when they are based on something well-known, because we have to know the original in order to appreciate the joke.

There are two kinds of parody:

1 A famous poem or passage re-written in a humorous way.

2 Something written in the style of a famous author or a particular type of story. The parody always 'sends up' (mocks) the original.

Re-writing famous pieces

There have been many parodies of the nursery rhyme, 'Mary had a little lamb'. For example:

Mary had a little dog
With little furry feet
And every lampost Mary passed
The dog was sure to greet.

Mary had a little lamb,
She also had a bear.
I've often seen her little lamb
But I've never seen her bear!

Write a parody of this nursery rhyme, or any other well-known rhyme. You must base it on the same rhythms and rhyme pattern as the original.

Parodies of style

Many writers enjoy writing parodies in the style of other authors' work, or parodying certain types of stories. The different types are known as 'genres'.

Some examples of genres:

Mystery fairy romance science-fiction western detective ghost adventure

We can usually recognise the genre from the way a story is written. For example, what kind of stories do you think these sentences might come from? How do you know?

- Once upon a time there was a princess who lived in a castle in a far away land.
- Black Jed stood facing the saloon. 'Come on out, Logan,' he hollered, 'we gotta score to settle, me 'n' you!'
- Their eyes met across the crowded room. Her heart skipped a beat as he approached and took her in his strong, manly arms.
- As the chimes of midnight echoed through the empty house, he heard a faint rustling on the landing. Then slowly, very slowly, the heavy oak door of his bedroom began to creak open.

It is quite easy to parody story genres if we know the typical sorts of things that happen and how they are usually described. We can call this *pastiche,* which is a kind of literary patchwork or collage. By sticking together characters, phrases and situations we have read about in stories of the same kind, we make a parody of the genre.

Write your own pastiche

Choose a story genre from the list above. Write down the typical kinds of people, names, places, objects, phrases and happenings you expect to find in such a story. Use some of these to help you create your storyline and imitate the style.

Figures of speech

English is full of expressions which often mean something different from what the words seem to say. For example, the following phrases all use colours. Do you know what they really mean, and can you think of any others?

Have you ever 'seen red', 'felt blue', been 'browned off', 'looked green about the gills', and 'argued that black is white'? Or are you 'in the pink' with a 'rosy future', and does 'every cloud have a silver lining'?

The two most important figures of speech are *similes* and *metaphors*. Similes and metaphors are more vivid ways of describing things and are particularly useful when writing poetry and stories.

Similes

Similes are expressions that compare two different things. They show us what is similar about them. They use the words 'like' or 'as'. For example:

The peach was *as smooth as a baby's bottom*.

On his first day at school he felt *like a fish out of water*.

His attempt at a joke went down *like a lead balloon*.

Make a collection of similes you know. You will be surprised how many there are. You will probably find that quite a few of them use colours or animals.

New similes

When we speak we often use similes like those above. However, poems and stories become far more interesting if we use similes we have made up ourselves. Once a phrase is well-known it usually becomes a *cliché*. Clichés are expressions that were once exciting and new, but have been repeated so often that they become dull and unoriginal.

Practise creating new similes by completing these phrases.

As wet as... As bumpy as...

She fell heavily to the floor like...

He ran round the field like...

Her nose was as long as...

Metaphors

Metaphors also use one thing to describe another, but they leave out the words 'like' and 'as'. Metaphors can come from all areas of life, such as food: 'life is just a bowl of cherries', or houses: 'an Englishman's home is his castle'.

Sport has given the language many metaphors. 'Throw in the towel', 'out for the count' and 'below the belt' all come from boxing. Cricket has given us 'knocked for six', 'caught out', 'stumped' and 'had a good innings'. The expression 'it's just not cricket' has come to mean anything which is not acceptable behaviour. Can you think of other sporting metaphors which have become part of everyday speech?

On the face of it...

Metaphors and similes are found in many expressions which can be funny if we take them literally. The following all use parts of the body.

- She's all fingers and thumbs.
- He's got two left feet.
- I've got a frog in my throat and butterflies in my tummy.
- He tied himself in knots trying to explain.

How many more can you find? Illustrate them literally. What do they really mean?

Doubletalk and disguise

Euphemisms

A euphemism is a way of saying something without having to call it by its real name. The main reason for doing this is to avoid sounding rude or offensive.

Some subjects always cause embarrassment. For example, people will use all sorts of expressions rather than say they are going to the 'lavatory' which they think sounds impolite. How many can you think of?

Death is another taboo subject, but more because we are afraid of it or do not want to hurt people by saying straight out that someone has died. You will hear expressions like these:

'passed away' 'fell asleep' 'gone to Jesus' 'departed this life' 'met his maker' 'kicked the bucket'

How many more have you heard?

Yet another reason to use a euphemism is to avoid having to say the truth about someone and offend them. We will go to some lengths rather than tell someone what we really think.

For example: *you're not ...*

fat - you're well-rounded and cuddly;

mean - you're just careful with your money;

drunk - you're just a little tired and emotional.

Political correctness

The twentieth century has seen a new kind of euphemism enter the language. *Political correctness* began in America and describes a way of trying to be positive and fair to different kinds of people who might be upset by certain words. For example: 'small' becomes 'vertically challenged'; 'poor' becomes 'economically disadvantaged'; 'disabled' becomes 'differently abled'; and 'ugly' becomes 'cosmetically different'. Politically correct terms are usually very long and unmusical in their sounds.

The wolf said, 'You know, my dear, it isn't safe for a little girl to walk through these woods alone.'

Red Riding Hood said, 'I find your sexist remark offensive in the extreme, but I will ignore it because of your traditional status as an outcast from society, the stress of which has caused you to develop your own, entirely valid, worldview. Now, if you'll excuse me, I must be on my way.'

(from *Politically Correct Bedtime Stories* by James Finn Garner)

Circumlocutions

Sometimes people try to hide the facts of what they are saying by using many words. You have to listen carefully to pick up the truth. Politicians, particularly, often do this. For example:

'With respect to the Honourable Member for -----, I have to say that, notwithstanding his spirited defence of the policy pursued by his government over the last few months, there is no doubt that there will be some people who will find that in replying to my question he has somehow failed to appreciate the full facts of this case'.

(This means 'you haven't answered the question and I think you're lying'.)

What do they really mean?

Can you uncover the real meaning of the following expressions?

She was wearing her birthday suit.

He was not in the first flush of youth.

You must have got out of the wrong side of the bed.

The actress said that she was just resting.

We had a robust exchange of views and a full and frank discussion.

Gender

There are four different genders in English grammar, and all nouns belong to one of them.

1. **Masculine** – male, such as *boy, man, king, hero, father*.
2. **Feminine** – female, such as *girl, woman, queen, heroine, mother*.
3. **Common** – living things which can be either male or female, such as *child, gardener, leader, singer, teacher, cat*.
4. **Neuter** – things that are neither male nor female, such as *chair, pen, house, book, spaghetti, dream, coffee*.

Can you think of more for each category?

Not all languages divide gender in the same way, and sometimes nouns can appear in unexpected categories. For instance, German has only three genders - masculine, feminine and neuter: der Baum (tree) is masculine; die Strasse (street) is feminine; but das Mädchen (girl) is neuter. French, however, has only two genders - masculine and feminine: le fantôme (ghost) is masculine, while la plume (pen) is feminine.

Odd ones out

Sometimes living things are called 'it' as if they were neuter, such as cats, dogs, other animals, and even children!

'What's the baby called?'

'It hasn't got a name yet'.

And lifeless things that should be neuter, sometimes become male or female. Here are some examples:

- Children's dolls, teddy bears, and other soft toys are often imagined to have human personalities. We even give them names and make up stories about them, such as 'Winnie the Pooh' and 'Paddington Bear'.
- Boats and cars are usually called 'she', particularly by male owners. Why might this be, do you think?
- Since ancient times in myths and legends some nouns have been thought to have male or female characteristics. Words that suggest power and strength are traditionally male, such as Death, Mountains, Sun and Old Father Time, while words that suggest beauty and gentleness are traditionally female, such as Moon, Peace, Liberty, Mother Nature and Mother Earth.

Feminism and Sexism

'A woman's place is in the home.'
'It's a man's life in the army.'

In the twentieth century, feminism has become an important political movement. It began in the USA and spread to other countries. The aim of feminism is to ensure that women have the same opportunities in life as men and enjoy equal worth and equal rights with men.

Throughout English history, men have usually been considered more important than women. Men did the 'important' jobs, such as ruling the country, fighting wars and earning a living. Women stayed at home doing the housekeeping, having children and looking after their men. This difference shows in many of the words and phrases of the language and has given us a new word - *sexism*.

Sexism describes remarks or actions which are unfair or degrading to either men or women. However, we usually apply it to expressions (said by men) which are unfair to women.

Changes in the language

Since the 1960s feminists have partially succeeded in getting rid of what was considered sexist language.

- Most job titles now contain the word 'person' (or other common nouns) so that they can apply to both men and women. For example:

  chairman is often now *chairperson* or even *chair* (neuter)

  dustman is frequently *refuse collector* (common)

  salesgirl has become *sales assistant* (common).

- Children's books no longer tend to show sexual stereotypes, such as mother in the kitchen and father working on the car.
- Ms. is now used alongside Miss and Mrs so that it is not always known if a woman is married.
- Instead of saying 'he', we now say 'he or she', or 'they'. Instead of 'his', we say 'his or her', or more usually 'their'. For example, we no longer say 'each visitor must give his name before he comes in', but 'each visitor must give his or her name before he or she comes in' or 'each visitor must give their name before they come in'.

How far will it go?

Some feminists would like to change all words and phrases which contain the words 'man', 'men' or 'his'.

Instead of wo**men** - wimmin.

Instead of **his**tory - herstory.

Many well-known expressions in English would have to change. For example:

mankind   the Family of **Man**   **man**handle
Stone-age **man**   **Man**'s best friend (dog)
over**man**ning   no **man** is an island   **man**power
an English**man**'s home is **his** castle

Can you think of more? Is it possible to find alternative expressions without sounding clumsy?

A female refuse collector.

Interesting oddities

Possibly the longest name given to a child in England was that recorded at the General Register Office in the nineteenth century. The surname was Pepper, but the Christian names ran through the alphabet!

Anna Bertha Cecilia Diana Emily Fanny Gertrude Hypatia Inez Jane Kate Louisa Maud Nora Ophelia Quince Rebecca Starkey Teresa Ulysis Venus Winifred Xenophon Yetty Zeus... Pepper.

In 1939, at the age of 67, a Californian called Ernest Vincent Wright published a novel called *Gadsby*. What was special about it was that none of its 50,110 words contained the letter 'e'. (The special name for a piece written without a particular letter of the alphabet is a *lipogram*.) 'E' is the most used letter of the English alphabet, so the novel was quite an achievement. How good it was as a novel is another matter altogether. Here is an extract.

> Upon this basis I am going to show you how a bunch of bright young folks did find a champion; a man with boys and girls of his own; a man of so dominating and happy individuality that Youth is drawn to him as is a fly to a sugar bowl. It is a story about a small town...

This advertisement appeared in *The Times* in 1842. The lady advertising for a job uses all the letters of the alphabet to describe herself!

> TO WIDOWERS AND SINGLE GENTLEMEN - WANTED by a lady, a SITUATION to superintend the household and preside at table. She is Agreeable, Becoming, Careful, Desirable, English, Facetious, Generous, Honest, Industrious, Judicious, Keen, Lively, Merry, Natty, Obedient, Philosophic, Quiet, Regular, Sociable, Tasteful, Useful, Vivacious, Womanish, Xantippish, Youthful, Zealous, &c.

When people cannot think of the word they want, they often use made-up nonsense words instead. Some of these sound quite amusing.

whachamacallit thingummyjig oojamaflip doobry thingummybob whatsit whatsitsname thingy doodah wosname thingybobby ooja

This sign is outside The Plough at East Hendred in Oxfordshire. Can you read what it says?

HERESTO PANDS PEN D ASOCI
AL HOU R INHAR M(LES SMIRT)
HA ND FUNLET FRIENDS.
HIPRE IGN BE JUSTAN DK
INDAN DEVIL SPEAKOF NO NE

Some people seem to have very appropriate names for their jobs or professions. Is it just by accident or can the name you have at birth determine what you will do in life? All these names are real.

- Reverend Christian Church
- Major Minor (US army)
- I.C. Shivers (iceman)
- A. Moron (Commissioner of Education)
- Cardinal Sin (Archbishop)
- Plummer and Leek (plumbers)
- Lawless and Lynch (lawyers)
- Mrs Screech (singing teacher)
- Justin Tune (chorister)
- Mr Vroom (motorcycle dealer)
- Groaner Digger (undertaker)
- Wyre and Tapping (detectives)
- Firmin A. Gryp (banker)

Macaronic verse mixes two languages together. This rhyme in what looks like Latin has been popular with Latin teachers in many a school. The best way to make sense of macaronic verse is to read it out loud - then you can hear what it is saying!

Caesar adsum iam forte,
Brutus et erat,
Caesar sic in omnibus,
Brutus in is at.

(Caesar (h)ad some jam for tea,
Brutus ate a rat,
Caesar's sick in omnibus,
Brutus in (h)is (h)at.)

The following is a line of macaronic language which looks as though it is in French. Say it out loud. Can you hear what is really being said - in English?

Pas de lieu Rhône que nous.